PRAISE FOR *OBNOXIOUS PARENTS AND RUTHLESS COACHES*

"Randy Corwin does a nice job explaining why you NEVER volunteer to umpire at a kid's game! Both amusing and instructive, parents of young athletes can learn a lot from these stories."
—Dan Shaughnessy, sports columnist for the *Boston Globe*, and author of *Senior Year* and *Wish it Lasted Forever: Life with the Larry Bird Celtics*

"We can all learn from amazing stories of well-intentioned parents and coaches causing themselves some very embarrassing moments. Youth sports teach children how to win, lose, and handle difficult situations. Parents should use the opportunity to teach our most precious youth these lessons the right way rather than showing them how to rant and rave. I highly recommend this book."
—Dave Wallace, former Boston Red Sox pitching coach and MLB front office executive

"All youth organizations should ask, better yet require, parents and coaches to read this book. Randy shares

amazingly scary situations from personal experiences of umpiring. People taking youth sports too seriously by involving themselves in officiating games are ruining it for all, especially the kids."
—Brenda Hilton, founder of Officially Human (info@officiallyhuman.com) and senior director of officiating, Big Ten Conference

OBNOXIOUS PARENTS AND RUTHLESS COACHES

OBNOXIOUS PARENTS AND RUTHLESS COACHES

TALES OF ADULTS TAKING YOUTH BASEBALL WAY TOO SERIOUSLY

Randy Corwin

The author has tried to recreate events, locations, and conversations from his/her memories of them. The author has made every effort to give credit to the source of any images, quotes, or other material contained within and obtain permissions when feasible.

Copyright © 2023 by Randy Corwin

All rights reserved. No part of this book may be reproduced or transmitted in any form or by any means, electronic or mechanical, including photocopying, recording, or any information storage and retrieval system, without permission in writing from the author.

ISBN: 978-1-6653-0593-8 - Paperback
eISBN: 978-1-6653-0594-5 - ePub

These ISBNs are the property of BookLogix for the express purpose of sales and distribution of this title. The content of this book is the property of the copyright holder only. BookLogix does not hold any ownership of the content of this book and is not liable in any way for the materials contained within. The views and opinions expressed in this book are the property of the Author/Copyright holder, and do not necessarily reflect those of BookLogix.

Library of Congress Control Number: 2023908555

⊗This paper meets the requirements of ANSI/NISO Z39.48-1992 (Permanence of Paper)

Cover artwork and cartoon illustrations by Brian Casey
Author Photo by Dan Corwin

053023

Dedicated to My Family

To my late parents, Herb and Norma Corwin, who gave me my love of baseball and writing, and to my sister, Laurie, who always kept a close eye on her little brother.

As lifelong, suffering, diehard Boston baseball fans, we were sick and tired of our archrivals from New York always winning. We dreamed that one day, we would be the champions. On October 27, 2004, it happened for the first time in eighty-six years. I'd waited forty-eight years. My dad had waited eighty. He died unexpectedly two weeks later. The last conversation we had was about how happy we were to have finally seen Boston's boys of summer win it all.

To my wonderful children, Jess and Dan, now wonderful adults. Coaching your teams was a blast and reminded me how much fun baseball can be.

To Janice, my wife, best friend, and "better half" since we were teenagers in the '70s. Thank you for putting up with me all these years, especially when you become a "baseball widow" for several months every year during the baseball season.

CONTENTS

Preface	WHEN I WAS A KID	ix
Introduction	HOW GROWN-UPS "SCREW IT UP"	xv
	WHY GROWN-UPS "SCREW IT UP"	xxviii
	SOME OF THE MANY WAYS GROWN-UPS "SCREW IT UP"	xx

TALES OF OBNOXIOUS PARENTS	**1**
TALES OF RUTHLESS COACHES	**65**
MY YEARS AS A COACH AND MANAGER	**133**
Acknowledgments	205

PREFACE
WHEN I WAS A KID

We've all heard the expression, "Things were different when I was a kid." It's true. I was a kid in the 1960s. Life was simpler then. Parents told us to "go out and play." So what did we do? We went out and played. We'd see other kids outside and join them. If we didn't see anybody, we'd knock on neighbors' doors and in no time, a bunch of kids were playing together outside.

Life's different now, and I'm not sure if it's better—or if people are happier. Today, many people never even bother to meet their neighbors. Kids don't just "go out and play" anymore. These days, your kids require an appointment to have someone to play with, known as a "playdate." Playdates are often made weeks in advance, though they may only last an hour.

It was a long time ago, but I can't recall ever knocking on a neighbor's door, asking my friend's parents, "Can Tommy come out and play?" only to be told, "Sorry, Randy, you need to make an appointment to play with Tommy, maybe in a week or two."

Kids today are too busy to just go out and play. Their schedule is booked solid. Parents think that the more activities they can cram into their child's life, the better the child will turn out.

In addition to school, kids play sports like baseball, football, basketball, soccer, lacrosse, hockey, swimming, gymnastics, tennis, etc. They do other activities, like dance, ballet, hip-hop, singing lessons, guitar, piano, trumpet, horseback riding, scouts, sports camps, etc. Activities available today are endless, which is great, but some parents feel their kids must do EVERYTHING!

My favorite kid's activity is "Yoga for Kids." This is probably so popular because kids need to decompress from all the stress caused by their well-meaning parents over-scheduling them to the point where they have no time left to be a kid. They have no time to just go out and play.

Life was simpler when I was a kid. Technology was coming but hadn't arrived yet. To communicate with relatives in other states, we wrote letters. My parents thought I was a cutting-edge, high-tech guru in 1965 when I used a tape recorder to make "talking letters" to mail to my grandparents. We watched black-and-white TV until I was twelve. We only had a few channels, and when we wanted to change the channel, we actually had to get up from the couch and turn the dial by hand. We never lost the remote control, because there wasn't one!

I thought I was happy. Maybe I didn't know any better. I didn't have the choices of activities available today—but I didn't care. I had baseball. I played other sports, but baseball was the one I loved. When I was seven or eight, I wasn't old enough to play in Little League, because you had to be nine. T-ball hadn't even been invented yet. I played baseball in the streets of our neighborhood with my friends. When school was out in the summer, my parents would pack me a lunch, and I'd ride my bike, with my glove on the handlebars, sometimes alone, sometimes with friends, almost a mile to my school's baseball field, where there were always a bunch of kids ready to play baseball.

There were no coaches with clickers tracking pitch counts. There were no parents to scream at umpires, and no umpires either! There were no grown-ups to ruin our fun. It was the best. It was just a bunch of kids playing baseball. Kids from seven to twelve years old all played together. The older kids ran things, but everyone took turns being team captains, which meant you picked the players for your team. There were no entire weekends spent on tryouts and evaluations, or endless hours spent drafting players for teams. There were two captains. One captain said, "I'll take Joey." The other captain said, "I'll take Billy." In two minutes, teams were picked, unlike the arduous project that assembling teams in today's youth leagues entails.

We played baseball all day, almost every day, all summer long. We never wanted to do anything else. Nobody had pools, belonged to country clubs, or even had air-conditioned homes. Was it hot out? I'm sure it was. Did we have arguments during our games? Probably, but I guess we worked things out. All I remember was leaving in the morning, riding my bike to the baseball field, and playing baseball all day. Everyone was supposed to be home for dinner by 6:00 p.m., and everyone always made it home safely and on time.

Nobody had cell phones, but our parents weren't worried. They knew where we were and what we were doing. It wasn't organized or supervised by adults. It was simple and fun. It was just a bunch of kids playing baseball.

Thinking about what the world is like today, I wonder why my parents never thought I'd get kidnapped, lured away by a pedophile, or abducted by aliens. They knew I'd show up at dinnertime and I always did. It is a different world today, however, and what I did then is unthinkable today. What sane parent would let their eight-year-old ride their bike, sometimes alone, a mile each way to a baseball field where they'd be gone all day without any method of contact?

Parents who do that today would be charged with child abuse and neglect. What parents did back then doesn't happen anymore. They left their sons alone and just let us be kids having fun playing baseball.

Technology was supposed to make our lives easier and better. When I was a kid, I only knew one family that had a home computer. Their name was *The Jetsons*. Every Saturday morning in the '60s, I'd watch this animated cartoon about a futuristic space-age family who had computers, cell phones, and even robots that cleaned their home. The stress in George Jetson's life with these inventions was off the charts. Who knew back then that these crazy gadgets would rule our lives just a few decades later?

Has technology made our lives better? It has—but while improving our lives, it has created problems as well. When kids think of technology, they think of video games, cell phones, and social media, all of which have taken over our lives. We've become a society of slaves to technology, spending every waking minute staring at the "devices" that define and run our lives.

Since kids today need appointments for playdates, whenever there's no playdate scheduled, there are always video games or a million things to do on their cell phones, which every kid over the age of three seems to own. Busy parents use video games or cell phones as babysitters. If there's no supervised activity or playdate scheduled, kids often spend the whole day playing video games or staring at their phones and eating junk food. Better living through technology? I'm not so sure.

Today's technology and lifestyles have changed what it's like to be a kid. Kids don't just go out and play baseball or anything else like we did when I was young. Everything kids do today, including playing baseball or any activity, is scheduled, organized, and run by grown-ups. Parents today mean well, and the overwhelming majority are great people. Unfortunately, a small minority of adults seem to go temporarily insane at times, completely failing as parents and role models when they take youth sports way too seriously and winning is all they care about.

All the kids care about is having fun! When I was a kid, my friends and I played baseball because it was fun, not to satisfy the needs of parents to watch us destroy our opponents.

With social media today, people can say whatever they want whenever they want, without fear of consequences. Nobody takes responsibility for anything, as there is always someone else to blame for whatever goes wrong in their lives. When you combine these attitudes with competitive personalities and unconditional love for children that parents so desperately want to succeed, this is a recipe for disaster.

When children play sports, the focus should be 100 percent on them, but too often parents and coaches make it more about themselves than the kids. Youth sports have become a bomb just waiting for a spark from overly competitive parents or coaches to ignite the fuse and trigger an explosion. When adults lose perspective of what's really important in life and what isn't, and "explode" during what are essentially meaningless youth games, impressionable children who want to be just like their parents when they grow up are watching.

What isn't important in life is when an adult thinks the umpire blew a "SAFE!" call at the plate that gave the other team the lead. Everyone will forget this ever happened the next day. What is important in life is having adults lead by example to show children the right way to react and conduct themselves when things don't go their way. When parents either lose it and go ballistic over a close, controversial play in a game, or keep their cool and accept what happened even if they disagree, the way parents react becomes permanently ingrained in the child's memory. They will never forget the behavior they saw, whether it was good or bad, and will grow up to be just like their parents.

Although the venomous wrath of an adult's explosive tirade is usually directed toward an individual—such as the umpire, opposing coach, or even some poor kid who dropped a fly ball—innocent bystanders who are in the wrong place at the wrong time become victims as well. The collateral damage done to children in youth sports who witness unacceptable conduct by the role-model adults they worship, imitate, and emulate is real and cannot be overlooked.

INTRODUCTION
HOW GROWN-UPS "SCREW IT UP"

Bob Lemon was a Hall of Fame pitcher in the 1940s and '50s. He once said, "Baseball was made for kids, and grown-ups only screw it up." He was right. The purpose of youth baseball, especially in recreational leagues, is to teach baseball skills, the value of teamwork, being part of something bigger than yourself, and promoting good sportsmanship, whether you win or lose. While kids just want to have fun, do their obnoxious parents and ruthless coaches often think winning is all that matters? Do grown-ups who are involved in youth baseball act like complete fools at times? Do grown-ups forget it's just kids playing a game? Do grown-ups forget that playing baseball is supposed to be fun?

The answers to these questions are YES, YES, YES, AND YES!

In this book, you'll read true stories of parents and coaches saying or doing bizarre and unbelievable things. Anyone who's coached, officiated, or been a parent of a young athlete has witnessed this insanity for themselves. Although these stories are all about baseball, it's a problem in all youth sports. Adults forget they are role models. While youth sports are just games, they teach valuable "life lessons" to those who participate. Players watch how their parents and coaches behave and conduct themselves accordingly.

Adults who don't behave properly at youth games need to calm down. Winning these games is not a matter of life and death. Youth games are not attended by college recruiters handing out scholarships, or by pro-scouts ready to ink ten-year-olds to zillion-dollar contracts.

I urge anyone who coaches or is a parent of a young athlete to heed this bit of advice: These are kids, not professional athletes. Teach them to try their best, respect the game, teammates, coaches, opponents, officials, and to just have fun. If this message gets across, everybody wins, regardless of the score. Don't be that guy or gal who takes youth games way too seriously, or your behavior may be documented in my next book!

As a youngster in the 1960s, I watched a police show on TV called *Dragnet*, where detectives Joe Friday and Bill Gannon always got the bad guy. At the beginning of each episode, the narrator would say, "The stories you are about to see are true. The names have been changed to protect the innocent."

Here, the stories you are about to read are also true. They have to be. You can't make this stuff up. There is one major difference, however, between *Dragnet* and this book. Here the names have been changed to protect THE GUILTY!

I personally experienced many of these stories, while others were told to me by parents, coaches, and umpires from all over the country. In many of these stories, the insatiable desire to win by adults was taken way too far. Instead of youth baseball games being focused entirely on the participants, they became more about the adults than the kids. My goal in telling these stories is that others will learn from their mistakes and not make the same ones.

Several times during my two-plus decades of coaching

and umpiring, after telling friends some crazy baseball story, they'd tell me, "Hey, someday you should write a book about this stuff." In 2012, my fortune cookie from a Chinese restaurant said, "Someday you will write a book." Fortune cookies never lie. "Someday" has finally arrived. I hope you enjoy reading this book as much as I've enjoyed writing it.

WHY GROWN-UPS "SCREW IT UP"

Grown-ups don't try to screw up youth baseball. They mean well. They love their children unconditionally, but this love is what makes grown-ups "screw it up." They can't just *let* their kids have fun. Adults must *make* their kids have fun. They try way too hard. Their mission is to create "baseball utopia." In their quest for a perfect baseball world for the children they love, parents complain about anything and everything. Coaches try too hard to win or show obvious favoritism toward their own kids. League organizers form political cliques among each other. Getting anything changed in league rules or policies practically requires an act of Congress, even when it makes obvious sense to change something. This is just about a bunch of kids playing baseball. It's a simple concept, but in their quest to make everything perfect for the kids they love, complicated rules are put into place along with complex bureaucracies to administer these rules.

Grown-ups "screw it up" because if they don't control everything, they think kids won't know how to have fun playing a kid's game. They work to achieve "baseball utopia," but instead, they screw it up.

When I was a kid, the adults left us alone. They just let a bunch of kids play baseball. We played without adults counting pitches. We played without adults only letting their own kids pitch. We played without adults screaming at umpires.

Maybe our parents were too busy working, or maybe they saw we were doing fine on our own. Perhaps they thought they'd screw it up if they tried to run everything for us. Were parents fifty years ago actually smarter than today's better-educated parents? Parents back when I was a kid just let us play. Today's parents can't do that. That's why they "screw it up."

SOME OF THE MANY WAYS GROWN-UPS "SCREW IT UP"

How do grown-ups screw it up? Let me count the ways. Grown-ups involved in youth baseball fall into several categories, each with slightly different job requirements:

1. Parents of players, who aren't coaches and don't help run the league—all their job entails is signing the player up, paying the fee, bringing them to games and practices, watching the games, and supporting their kid and team. This doesn't sound like a difficult job, does it? How can they possibly screw this up?
2. Managers and assistant coaches, whose job is to organize and run a team of usually ten to twelve players. Each team plays in an age group division of around five to ten teams, depending on the size of the league. Teams usually play around twenty games over a couple of months.

   In most "recreational leagues" the emphasis is not supposed to be on winning. The job of managers and assistant coaches, who are usually also parents of players on the team, is to teach fundamentals, equally divide playing time, and give players the chance to play different positions.

Although winning is supposedly not the priority, team standings are kept, and looked at by some coaches on an hourly basis. Playoffs are conducted at the end of the season, and the winner gets a big trophy and bragging rights. The problem is that you can't tell coaches they shouldn't care about winning and then put in place tremendous incentives to win. You're a hero if you finish first, and an incompetent buffoon if you finish last.

What a dilemma! How could anything possibly be easier to screw up than this?

3. League organizers (commissioner, president, secretary, treasurer, etc.) run the league. Also known as "The Board," they take care of money, run tryouts, make rules, choose teams, etc. They often take tasks that could be quick and easy and turn them into complicated, time-consuming projects. Board members spend a lot of time together, putting in long hours to make a league run. Strong friendships and political "cliques" often develop among them.

Did I say **politics**? What could **politics** possibly NOT screw up?

Let's examine what parents, coaches, and league organizers do to screw up and complicate a simple kid's game.

TALES OF OBNOXIOUS PARENTS

"THE COMPLAINERS"

Most town recreational leagues are run entirely by unpaid volunteers. Almost all of these volunteers have children who play in the league. Of the parents who don't coach or help run the league, most are terrific, with 90 percent being friendly, supportive, and appreciative of the time coaches and league organizers put in to make youth baseball a great experience. Unfortunately, 10 percent ruin it for the other 90 percent. These 10 percent are what I call "the complainers."

The good lord must have put these people on earth for one purpose. Their sole purpose in life is to complain. They never volunteer to help with anything but complain about everything done by those who do volunteer. They complain about how much playing time their kid gets. They complain he plays certain positions too often and doesn't play other positions often enough. They complain the coach tries too hard to win or doesn't try hard enough to win. They complain when the weather's too hot and when the weather's too cold. Today they complain because it's raining, and tomorrow they'll complain when the sun's in their eyes. They complain that two games a week aren't enough, three games a week are too many, and the teams aren't put together fairly. When they can't think of baseball stuff to complain about, they can always complain about overcooked hot dogs at the concession stand.

Of course, none of these complainers would ever volunteer to help with anything. They claim they have no time to help. They say they're too busy. They're right. There is no time left in their day. They've spent their whole day complaining.

"I NEVER, EVER COMPLAIN, BUT... (TWO PAGES LATER)"

Most complaints in youth sports are minor and are taken care of with a quick call to the appropriate coach or board member of the league. Some complaints, however, get taken to the next level. Sometimes complainers are so upset they put their complaints in writing. This is serious stuff! My favorite complainers are the ones who try to make it sound like they never complain about anything, before lodging their complaints. They preface their complaint with "I've never written a complaint before *but*," followed by a lengthy, multipage dissertation that could only be written by a seasoned veteran complainer with years of high-level complaining experience under their belt.

For many years, I supervised a group of teenagers who umpired games played by seven-to-twelve-year-olds. Most feedback was positive, just minor complaints now and then. Not this time. This complaint featured everything this irate mom could throw at me—and it was quite entertaining.

It was the day after a semifinal summer league game for the nine-year-old division. Bear with me, this complaint is lengthy, and this is the condensed version!

"Good morning, I hope you are having a great summer!"

(For some reason she started off trying to be nice before making an all-out effort to ruin my great summer.)

She went on to write, "I have a 'SHORT COMPLAINT' about the umpire at last night's game, who I was told is seventeen. First, I want to make it clear that I NEVER, EVER complain about umpires no matter how bad they are. Usually, if the umpires are terrible, they are terrible for both teams. But last night, it was different. Our team, which had been CRUSHING the competition every game, almost lost the game because the ump was so bad. But he was only bad for us. He was fine for the other team. It was a TRAVESTY! He wouldn't call strikes for our pitchers like he would for their pitchers, even when our pitches were perfect. I felt so bad for our pitchers that I started yelling, 'Nice pitch!' or 'Good one!' before the ump made his calls because I could clearly see that the pitches were strikes even though this terrible umpire kept calling them balls."

On and on and on she went, and mercifully, two pages later, closed her "short complaint" with, "I hope you don't brush me off as just another complaining parent, because I'm not a complainer." Her final line was, "That's it, I'm done complaining. Enjoy the rest of the summer."

A two-page complaint from this mom was very impressive, given her repeated claims that she wasn't a complainer, and has NEVER, EVER complained about anything before. While I don't like to call anyone a liar, she complained so eloquently about this "travesty" inflicted upon her nine-year-old and his team, that I highly suspected this wasn't her first rodeo. Did she really think these poor kids couldn't "crush" their opponent like they did every other game because of an umpire who was bad, but only bad for their team?

Of course, in her mind, it was all the umpire's fault because his strike zone was too small for her team's pitchers, but not for the other team.

She received from me an equally lengthy response: (This is the abridged version)

> Dear _____:
>
> I'm sure you're aware of how difficult umpiring a nine-year-old's baseball game can be. Although they aren't perfect, our youth umpires are very capable. By employing local teenagers who played in our league when they were younger, we provide jobs to our former players. If we used adult umpires, the cost to the league would be higher and each family would pay more to have their kids play baseball.
>
> As a parent, think of how difficult this would be on your son if he becomes an umpire when he's older. Picture him on a hot summer night, working a game of nine-year-olds where the quality of baseball is not very good. There's one group of parents taking the game way too seriously to his left, and another group of parents taking the game way too seriously to his right. Don't forget the coaches, on both sides, who also take the game way too seriously. With every call of "ball" or "strike," half the place disagrees, and comments from "umpires in the stands" like yourself are heard loud and clear.
>
> In addition to being distracting to the umpire, making comments of "Nice one!" or "Good pitch!" before the umpire makes his call is a

blatant violation of our parents' and spectators' "Code of Conduct" while watching our games.

Parents and coaches who are thirty to sixty feet away, off to the side, and looking through a fence think they can see balls and strikes from there, but they can't.

If you could, we'd put umpires in the dugouts or bleachers where they wouldn't be constantly hit by foul balls or pitches the catcher can't catch!

The umpire who worked your game usually umpires games for eleven-to-twelve-year-olds, and if he used too small a strike zone for the nine-year-olds, I apologize. He has been spoken to and the problem will not be repeated. I must, however, call into question your accusation that the umpire was biased against your team, and that he called the game differently for one team than he did for the other. I assure you, he had nothing against your team. Umpires rarely determine who wins a game, especially at this level of baseball. Please feel free to contact me if you wish to discuss this further.

Enjoy the rest of your summer! [Figured I could also at least pretend to be nice!]

I never heard from her again and was just fine with that.

THE BIGGEST BUSH-LEAGUE COMPLAINT

Sometimes complaints you hear as an umpire make you shake your head when parents say things that make no sense whatsoever. In the bottom half of the final inning of a fourteen-year-old Babe Ruth game, the home team, down by one run with two outs, had the tying run on first base. The batter hit a gap shot between the left and center fielders. I was an umpire and noticed that, as the batter rounded first base on his way to second, he missed first base by at least two feet and stopped at second with a stand-up double. The runner scored from first to tie the game. The home crowd was going wild as the game was now tied with the winning run on second base!

I wondered if the first baseman or anyone on the visiting defensive team noticed and would appeal that the batter who hit the double missed first base. (In this situation, umpires don't say anything about a missed base unless a defensive coach or player notices and makes "an appeal" to an umpire before a pitch is thrown to the next batter.) The first baseman didn't notice, but somebody in the crowd yelled to the manager, "Hey, Jack, the batter missed first base!" Immediately the manager said to me and the other umpire, "We are appealing that the runner on second missed first base." The ball was then thrown by the pitcher to the first baseman, who stepped on first base.

Since the batter missed first base and became "out number three" on the appeal, the game-tying run didn't count and suddenly the game was over. The crowd was stunned, and an angry mom jumped up and yelled out, "YOU CAN'T END A GAME LIKE THIS!"

As the other umpire and I walked off the field toward the parking lot, we had to pass by some spectators, who were all fairly quiet, still shocked at how the game ended. Suddenly, the same woman who'd informed us that we couldn't "end a game like this," decided to enlighten us even more.

As we were about to walk past her, she jumped up, got right in my face, and angrily barked, "THE HOME TEAM CAN'T LOSE A GAME BECAUSE OF A CALL LIKE THAT. NOBODY EVER ENFORCES MISSED BASES. THAT WAS THE BIGGEST BUSH-LEAGUE CALL I'VE EVER SEEN!"

A bit surprised by this confrontational mom, I was thinking:

1. "YOU (meaning the umpires) can't end a game like this?" What did the umpires do wrong?
2. Was it the fault of the umpires that this player ran by first base without touching it? Were we supposed to pretend not to notice?
3. Are the umpires expected to give the home team a break and not require them to touch the bases like the visiting team has to?
4. "Nobody ever enforces missed bases," seriously?

Trying to be diplomatic, I replied while still walking, "I'm sorry your team lost but the batter missed first base by at least two feet. I'm sure you know one of the rules of baseball is you actually have to touch the bases, not just run by them."

She had no response for me.

Yes, it was a tough way for the home team to lose the game. No complaints from players or coaches, so parents have to jump in to "screw it up." Maybe she really thought it was the biggest bush-league call, but if anything, it was the biggest bush-league complaint!

"I'M A DOCTOR, DAMMIT!"

This parent encounter reminded me of the original *Star Trek* TV series. Whenever Captain James T. Kirk would ask the doctor of the starship *Enterprise* to perform some impossible surgery on a crew member who'd been blown to bits in an explosion and was near death, Dr. McCoy would bark back at Captain Kirk, "I'm a doctor, dammit! Not a magician!"

When managing a team of nine-year-olds, I met the father of one of my players for the first time. I didn't know he was a doctor. His complaint to me was unique. He didn't complain about anything baseball related. He complained about the way I addressed him. He came to pick up his son after practice one day and, having never met him, I introduced myself.

I said, "Hi, Mr. Higgins, I'm Randy. It's nice to meet you."

His response was not quite what I was expecting, which might have been something like, "Hi, Randy, I'm Fred Higgins, and it's nice to meet you too." You know, a normal, uneventful, everyday type of introduction, totally devoid of drama.

Instead, he barked back, just like Dr. McCoy would do to Captain Kirk, "I'M A DOCTOR, DAMMIT! I worked very hard to become a doctor and would appreciate you addressing me as DOCTOR Higgins."

A bit taken aback by this unexpected response, I almost countered with, "What the hell is your problem?" I think I did very well avoiding my temptation to respond with that, or something even better, such as: "I'm sure you worked very hard to become a doctor. Did you also work very hard to become a complete a--hole, or does that just come naturally to you?"

Instead, I wimped out, swallowed my pride, and took the high road. "Sorry, DOCTOR Higgins it is from now on. It was nice to meet you."

I don't think we ever spoke again, and my one, short conversation with the very charming DOCTOR Higgins was more than enough for me.

"YOU'RE PSYCHOLOGICALLY DAMAGING ONE OF MY TWINS"

(Contributed by David in Texas)

When coaching ten-year-olds in 2015, David from Texas had two players that were identical twins, named Mike and Ike. They looked and sounded alike. David had trouble telling them apart until they played baseball. While Ike was a terrific player, Mike wasn't very good, and really didn't want to be there. Although David tried to play everyone as equally as possible, the better twin played the more important positions more often.

Halfway through the season, David got an email from their father, saying that "Mike was becoming 'psychologically damaged' from not being treated the same as his twin brother."

David didn't really know what to say, but responded with:

"Your boys are identical twins, but their ability to play baseball and attitudes toward the game are completely different. Mike doesn't seem to even like baseball, while Ike loves it. I'll try to play them more equally, but that's not always possible. I'm sure there's a rivalry between twins, and there probably are other things Mike is better at than his brother."

David never heard back from their father. Ike continued playing baseball for a few more years, while Mike stopped at the age of ten. They were both good students, but Mike was a better student than his baseball-superior brother. Years later, Mike went on to become his high school senior class valedictorian, so apparently, he recovered from the "psychological damage" David inflicted on him at ten years old!

THE "RED CUP CROWD"

(Contributed by Paul from California)

When renowned chef Emeril Lagasse wants to spice up one of his dishes, he says, "Let's kick it up a notch!" Alcohol, obnoxious parents, and youth baseball don't mix. What happens when parents who take youth baseball way too seriously knock down a few "cold ones" during the game? The obnoxious scale gets kicked up a notch. Sometimes two or three notches!

Paul umpires in a California community that touts their parents as "passionate baseball fans." We'll call them obnoxious parents. Their big diamond has lights, and night games are played every weekend. In this town, Fridays and Saturdays are party nights, and having to watch their fourteen-year-olds play baseball does not stand in the way of happy hour.

Referred to by Paul as the "Red Cup Crowd," these are nocturnal creatures. They only come out at night, congregating on bleachers behind the backstop. Under cover of darkness, using minimal or no effort to be discreet, they reach into coolers, pouring drinks into sixteen-ounce plastic red cups, like those used at backyard barbecues. It's anyone's guess what's in the coolers. It could be beer, wine, or if it's close to Cinco de Mayo, maybe a pitcher of margaritas. Definitely not soda-pop!

As games progress, the "Red Cup Crowd" gets rowdier. On close pitches or plays, they come alive with cheers or boos, and sometimes yell at the umpire. Even conflicts among themselves can break out. One night, Paul heard a "well-hydrated" woman and man loudly arguing back and forth, and she shouted at him, "Oh, yeah, you big, tough guy, what are you gonna do, beat me up?"

The count was 3-2 on the batter, and all Paul could think about were these two "Red Cuppers" who sounded like they were about to kill each other. He called "TIME!" and stopped the game.

Paul called both managers over and told them to accompany him. With the two managers escorting him, everyone in the crowd was told that if they can't behave, the game would end, and both teams would forfeit.

That sobered them right up! They didn't want the party to end early, so they somewhat behaved for the rest of the game. I don't know why drinking at a fourteen-year-old's baseball game is necessary or allowed, but for some reason in this laid-back California town, the league ignores it.

That was Paul's last weekend-night game there. There would be no more "Red Cup" games on his schedule!

THE PUSHERS AND GRINDERS

I am firmly convinced that having children who play sports gives grown-ups a second chance for glory. Anyone who played youth sports as a kid likely dreamed of playing for their favorite pro team. In my case, I wanted to play baseball for Boston, and crush homers over the big green wall in left field. This dream fizzled out for me, and reality reared its ugly head when I was eleven or twelve and could still barely hit the ball out of the infield, never mind out of the park. Many adults loved the game but were not great baseball players as kids.

Many years later, as parents of kids that show "talent," they can push and grind their talented kids all the way to free college and a pro career. This is the parent's chance to relive their own failed childhood athletic career through their children, and nothing will stop them from making sure their "little Johnny" makes it to the top.

Parents often steer their kids into activities they once participated in, like baseball, soccer, football, dancing, tennis, swimming, singing, acting, etc. When kids get involved in sports or activities, parents take notice when their child shows some natural ability in said activity. They may have a good throwing arm, be a terrific skater, swim faster, or sing better than most kids their age.

Upon seeing even the smallest amount of "talent," parents' minds immediately start spinning out of control. Even though a kid might only be eight, fantasies of college scholarships and multimillion-dollar pro contracts take over the parent's mind, body, and soul. While deep down they know the odds are less than a million to one that their eight-year-old could play professional baseball, they are blinded by talent and the fantasy of it all. They think their kid is the exception, the one in a million that will make it to the pros. At eight years old, they run faster or hit better than any of their friends. Once talent is seen, they push and grind their son or daughter to make them the great athlete they never were. They make their kid practice constantly, whether they want to or not! Practicing regularly is great, but you need to know when to stop, and just let a kid be a kid. Some parents push and grind talented young athletes so hard, they give up the sport because it becomes more work than fun.

THE BUSINESS OF "BETTER" YOUTH BASEBALL

As an umpire, I work games with kids playing baseball in high-priced AAU or "club" teams. Playing on these teams can cost their parents thousands of dollars a year. These programs offer better coaching, nicer uniforms, more games, and higher caliber games than local town leagues. It's great for kids who want to eat, breathe, and sleep baseball. In these highly competitive leagues, winning is the top priority.

Years ago, when AAU teams had tryouts, they only took the very best players, the "cream of the crop." Many more players were cut than selected. If you were selected for one of these teams, you were truly an exceptional baseball player.

In recent years, despite the high cost, many more parents have wanted their kids to play on these teams either instead of or in addition to their local town league. While the number of players participating in local town recreational leagues is down in some communities, the number of available competitive club teams to play on has exploded. Parents who think their child has "talent" are willing to spend heavily to get the most out of that talent. The cost is hefty, sometimes $2,000–$4,000 or more versus $200 or less per season to play in their local league. In the past, when only the very best players were selected, good players were being cut and big bucks of parents willing to invest in their talented future stars were being turned away.

So, what happened? The club teams got smart and made a bold business decision. Why should they keep turning away all this money parents are lining up to give them? It's a business, and I can't blame them at all.

Now that there are so many club teams out there, while tryouts are still held, many more players today make the cut. If a parent has the money, and the player is at least decent but not "the best of the best," they'll be placed on the club's "B" team, while the best players make the "A" or "Elite" team. As a youth umpire, I work a lot of AAU games. While the higher-level games often do have very good players and very good quality baseball, some of the lower-level games are barely better than games with two average town league teams, but at a much higher price tag.

OBNOXIOUS PARENTS PAYING BIG BUCKS

As an umpire, you hear moans and groans. Parents' behavior in recreational leagues often goes well beyond moans and groans. In competitive leagues, bad-parent behavior is clearly "kicked up a notch." Parents pay thousands of dollars for their children to play on club teams and expect their teams to win. Although you hear some grumbling from coaches, they generally know enough to exercise restraint, so they don't get tossed out. The complaints umpires listen to in these games come far more often from the parents: "C'MON, BLUE! ["Blue" is another way to address the umpire.] HOW COULD THAT BE A STRIKE? HOW COULD THAT BE A BALL? HOW COULD HE BE OUT? IT WASN'T EVEN CLOSE!" They pay big money, and some expect every call to go their way. It's not unusual in these competitive leagues for umpires to ask coaches to speak to an unruly parent or for umpires to eject parents from games.

Umpires completely understand that parents, especially those paying big money for their young star to play on a high-priced team, are much better qualified to make accurate calls on close plays than umpires are. Just because they're sitting in a chair at a bad angle, 150 feet from the play, while looking through a chain-link fence, a bunch of players, and a cloud of dust, it doesn't matter to these obnoxious parents. Parents think they're better positioned and more qualified to make calls from where they sit than the umpire can. As umpires, we ignore it and laugh to ourselves, until they get out of hand.

More than once, I've stopped a game, walked over to the father (sometimes moms are worse!) who's had way too much to say, and suggested, "Sir, let's switch spots. You can take my place behind the plate, and I'll sit in your chair and yell at you constantly. Would you like to do that?" The handful of times I've done this, the loudmouth parent backed right down and apologized, completely embarrassed because the other parents were all laughing at him. In the rare event that he'd say anything more, he'd be told that if he continued, he would be asked to leave the premises. That almost always works, but on one memorable occasion, it didn't.

THE OBNOXIOUS AND DEFIANT PARENT

Embarrassing an obnoxious parent with the previously mentioned technique usually worked for me, but once, it didn't. After suggesting to an outspoken parent that we trade places, he came right back at me with, "If you'd just do your job like you're supposed to, I wouldn't be saying anything to you."

"Sir," I said. "Since you're going to tell me I'm not doing my job, I'm going to tell you you're not doing yours. Your job is to sit and watch the game, support your son and his team, and keep your opinions about officiating to yourself. If you can't do your job, I'll have no choice but to ask you to leave, and this is your first and last warning. Am I making myself clear?"

A simple "Yes" would have sufficed, but since he pays big money for his son to play on this team, he continued with, "I pay a lot of money for my son to play here. I can say whatever I want whether you like it or not, and you're doing a crappy job of umpiring."

"Okay, we're done here," I said. "I want you to leave."

"I'm not leaving," he shouted back, "and what are you going to do about it? Call the cops on me?"

"I could do that," I said, "but they really don't like being called in to handle parents who can't behave at their kid's baseball game. What's going to happen is if you don't leave right now and go sit in your car for the rest of the game, the game will end, and your son's team will forfeit. Should I ask the players, coaches, and other parents if they'd like to forfeit the game because you're refusing to leave?"

Upon hearing that, he got up and left and sat in his car in the parking lot for the rest of the game. After the inning was over, the team manager said to me, "Hey, I'm sorry about that guy. I'm glad you tossed him. He's sometimes been a pain in the ass to me too. His son's a good kid, but I never would have put him on my team if I had any idea his dad was like that. I also don't know what he was griping about. Trust me, I've seen some bad umpires, and you're doing fine."

He was one of the obnoxious parents I've dealt with who "kicked it up a notch." For most parents, just being obnoxious is enough, but since he was spending big bucks for his son to play on this team, he wanted to get his money's worth! He was both obnoxious AND defiant!

PARENTS MAKING KIDS PLAY TOO MUCH BASEBALL

Even for kids that love the game, there comes a point where it's just too much baseball. I once spoke to an eleven-year-old who played for both a club team and his town team—which was a lot of baseball. He had games or practices virtually every day, even having to be with both teams on the same day at times. His parents often shuttled him from one game or practice to another immediately after the first one ended. I asked him why he played so much baseball. His answer was, "My parents want me to play in both leagues. The AAU games are better, but there's too much pressure in them. The town games are a lot more fun."

Is it just me, or is there something wrong here? For an eleven-year-old, baseball should be fun, not "too much pressure."

FOR SOME PARENTS, EVEN BEING THE BEST ISN'T GOOD ENOUGH

(Contributed by Arnie from Florida)

Before I heard this story, I never imagined that a parent would push an eight-year-old to excel in a sport so hard that it bordered on abuse. Unfortunately, some parents are never satisfied, no matter what their kid does. If he struck out one batter, he should have struck out the side. If he hit a double, it should have been a triple. If he hit the ball over the fence by ten feet, it should have been by thirty feet.

In 2014, when Arnie's son was eight, he managed his recreational league team in Florida. The quality of baseball was really bad, but there were some standouts with obvious talent. One, since he was five, was the star athlete in every sport. He'd score eight to ten goals in soccer games, literally running circles around everyone. He often played sports with older kids because playing with kids his own age was a joke. On the diamond, nobody his age could approach his ability to throw or hit a baseball.

His father was his coach and was the ultimate "pusher and grinder." He'd scream incessantly at his son, who was always the star of the game, to do even better. No matter how good he was, it was never good enough. He'd push and grind his son like nothing Arnie had ever seen.

Watching games involving seven- and eight-year-olds is painful. Getting anybody out is an accomplishment. Getting anybody out with a well-executed baseball play is rare. As for double plays, keep dreaming. At this age, it's a comedy of errors, one after another. Arnie's team had a runner on first base. With the superstar at shortstop and Arnie's runner on first base, a ground ball was hit to the left of the shortstop.

Completely effortlessly, with the skill and poise of a much older player, he scooped up the grounder, and in one fluid motion glided to his left, stepped on second, and fired to first to complete the double play. The throw was chin high, not perfect, but caught easily by the first baseman. This was a beautifully executed baseball play! After an hour of watching endless walks, and errors upon errors, all spectators, and even the players, coaches, and parents of Arnie's team jumped up and applauded the great double play this eight-year-old had just turned against them!

Everyone watching the game was ecstatic, with one exception. His father stood up, screaming angrily at his son over the thunderous applause, "HOW MANY TIMES HAVE YOU BEEN TOLD TO HIT THE FIRST BASEMAN IN THE CHEST WITH THE THROW?" The crowd watching the game started laughing, thinking this guy was obviously joking.

But almost immediately, the crowd went silent. Deadly silent. You could hear a pin drop where seconds before the cheering was deafening. His father wasn't joking. He was completely serious. The player and everyone watching knew it. Stunned people in the crowd shook their heads in disbelief and disgust. He had made the only double play in the history of the seven- and eight-year-old league, but his throw to first, although caught easily by the first baseman, was chin high instead of chest high. Arnie saw the player's eyes welling up, but he fought off the tears because he wouldn't dare show weakness in front of his father. This kid was a great athlete. He knew it, was cocky about it, and was sometimes a bit of a bully to less talented players. For that reason, Arnie never liked him, but at that moment, when this sensational play just wasn't good enough to please his father, Arnie felt sorry for him. It seemed like other kids, even some who'd been bullied by this young star, felt sorry for him as well.

THE MEDDLING PARENT

(Contributed by Mike from Wisconsin)

As a coach, you interact with the parents of your players. In recreational baseball, coaches should give everyone equal playing time, and the chance to play all positions. A fair coach will do that if someone can play a position properly and safely. To pitch, you need to throw the ball forty-six feet, and doing it accurately is a bonus. You must also be able to catch the ball to protect yourself if a ball is hit to you. To play first base, you must catch the ball when another fielder throws it to you. As a coach, you don't want to put a player who can't catch the ball in a position where they could get badly hurt.

When coaching seven- and eight-year-olds in Wisconsin in 2012, Mike had some players whose parents really wanted their sons to play baseball but didn't take the time to teach them basic skills. One player had no idea how to catch a baseball and, consequently, was afraid of the ball.

Just like the "complainer" who prefaced her multipage written complaint about an umpire with "I never complain, but . . ." the father of Mike's player who was afraid of the ball approached Mike between innings of a game.

"Hey, coach," he said. "I don't want to be a meddling

parent, but I think it would really help his confidence if you'd let Carleton play first base."

Instead of responding with, "Don't be an idiot, how's getting hit in the face with a ball he can't catch going to help his confidence?" Mike's reply was more diplomatic like, "I can't play Carleton there because he doesn't catch the ball very well and we have some kids who throw pretty hard to the first baseman. I'm sorry, I won't take a chance on him getting hit in the face with a ball, it's just not a good idea."

The parent replied back, "Well, he's my son and I'm willing to take that chance."

After holding up the game going back and forth with this meddling parent who insisted he didn't want to be a meddling parent, Mike repeated his feelings of it being a really bad idea. Against his better judgment, to get the "meddling parent" off his back, Carleton was put at first base. Mike's assistant coach, knowing Carleton couldn't catch the ball, asked Mike, "Why are you putting him at first base?"

"Don't even ask," was Mike's answer.

The first batter hit a slow roller right at Carleton, a simple "just scoop up the ball and step on first base" play. It was the perfect confidence booster that young Carleton's meddling parent was hoping for. The ball rolled right through his legs. E3! (That's baseball-talk for an error charged to the first baseman.) I'm sure making an error on a play his grandmother could have made was a HUGE boost to his confidence.

The next batter hit a grounder to the pitcher, who made a good throw to first. Carleton got in position with his foot on the base, his glove stretched out, ready to catch the throw. The ball hit his glove and fell to the ground as the batter crossed first base. Another E3! He must've been exploding with confidence by now.

The next batter grounded to shortstop, and the throw to first was again a good one, and bounced right off his glove again! Three batters, three errors—Dad, your kid's confidence is soaring!

Thankfully, the next three batters struck out, so at least Carleton survived the inning with only his confidence shattered and not his teeth. Carleton's baseball career ended when he was nine because he thought "baseball wasn't fun."

THE SECOND COMING OF RANDY JOHNSON (THE DELUSIONAL PARENTS)

(Contributed by Harry from Arizona)

Parents who take youth sports too seriously can be called obnoxious for a variety of reasons. Some only care about winning, and some are downright mean to their kids if they don't play well. Some complain about everything all the volunteers who run the league do while they never offer to help. Some constantly scream at officials. Other obnoxious parents think their child is so good, they can only be described as completely delusional. Because of their unconditional love and dreams of success they have for the child they created, they see greatness. They see greatness, which nobody else can see, both in the current level of skills and the future potential of their child. The reason nobody else can see this greatness is because it exists only in the mind of the delusional parent.

In 2006, Mr. and Mrs. Johnson were 100 percent convinced that their nine-year-old son, Robbie, was a terrific pitcher now, and a sure bet to be a future major leaguer. Mr. Johnson talked to Harry, his son's coach, at the team's first practice, explaining how Robbie "attacks hitters."

Comparing his son to the Hall of Famer, he said to Harry,

"You know how Randy Johnson gets batters to expect a fastball but crosses them up with an unhittable slider? My RJ [Robbie] does the same thing, except he's too young to throw sliders. He starts them off with a first-pitch fastball and, once the batter's thinking fastball, delivers a DEVASTATING CHANGEUP that's a guaranteed swing and miss every time!"

Harry said the funniest thing about their conversation was how serious this guy was. He proclaimed his son's pitching mechanics were identical to one of the most dominant left-handers to ever pitch. He made such a big deal about his son being a lefty, talking about his pitching prowess like he was the second coming of Randy Johnson. Since the family's last name was also Johnson, his parents nicknamed their son "RJ," like the Hall of Famer was called. Robbie was four-foot-three, fifty pounds soaking wet, and could barely reach the plate from the mound. The only resemblance between this tiny kid and the six-foot-ten pitcher, also known as "The Big Unit," was that they both threw left-handed.

Most times, when parents really think their nine- or ten-year-old is a future pro, they are blinded by their child's talent if they are far superior to everyone they play with or against. In this case, in the eyes of everyone except his parents, Robbie was an average player at best.

"Devastating changeup," seriously?

When his son pitched, Dad sat in the stands and gave "signs" for what to throw. Robbie's mom cheered loudly for her son the entire game. Robbie looked at his dad before every pitch, and Dad called for fastballs, changeups, sinkers, splitters, two-seamers, four-seamers, etc. Every pitch looked the same to Harry, like a "MEATBALL!"

Let's get something straight: Nine-year-old batters do not "think fastball," or quiver at the thought of, "Uh-oh, what should I do when he throws me that devastating changeup?" They don't complicate things like adults do. All batters think about at this age are four simple questions:

1. Is the pitch going to hit me?
2. Is the pitch over my head?
3. Is the pitch in the dirt?
4. Is the pitch a mile outside?

With the pitch on the way, if the answer is no to these four questions, the batter will probably swing. No need to complicate things. Baseball is a simple game.

Randy Johnson's fastball had been clocked as high as 102 miles per hour. Robbie's pitches struggled to reach the plate from the mound. His fastball rocked the radar guns at sixteen miles per hour! His "devastating changeup" was probably fourteen miles per hour and didn't look a whole lot different from the fastballs, sinkers, and splitters that Dad would call for from the stands.

Randy Johnson retired from professional baseball in 2009, after a twenty-two-year career and was inducted into the Baseball Hall of Fame in 2015. Despite the prediction by Robbie's delusional parents that their RJ would follow in the footsteps of the original RJ, Robbie couldn't even make his high school team. Even though everyone else saw Robbie as a mediocre baseball player, his parents still saw greatness. They truly believed that their RJ possessed the most "devastating changeup" that the baseball world would, unfortunately, never see.

PARENTS WHO "MAKE THEIR KIDS PLAY"

(Contributed by Bruce in New Jersey)

For quarterbacks in pro football, Tom Brady was the G. O. A. T. (Greatest of All Time). If the same designation was available for dads, the undisputed G. O. A. T. for dads would be Ward Cleaver from the 1960s family sitcom, *Leave It to Beaver*. Whenever one of his sons had a problem and needed fatherly advice, Ward Cleaver always knew exactly what to say, and how to say it.

In youth sports, some kids play who clearly don't want to, because their parents insist on it and "make them play" anyway. Usually, if the kid complains enough, most parents let them stop playing after a season or two.

In 2018, a fellow coach in Bruce's son's league was a baseball-loving fanatic who couldn't understand why his son had no interest in the game, and "made him play." This ten-year-old told everyone, "I hate baseball and only play because my dad makes me."

After a game, Bruce's son left his bat in a dugout at the field, so Bruce went back later to grab it. It looked like nobody was at the field, but as he approached the back of the dugout, he heard and recognized two voices. One was the baseball-fanatic coach, the other his baseball-hating son, who was crying his eyes out. The back of the dugout was

enclosed, so they couldn't see Bruce coming, and didn't know he was there. Bruce stopped and waited quietly so he wouldn't disturb this important father-son dialogue.

"EVERYBODY ON THE TEAM SAYS I SUCK!" the ten-year-old cried out to his father/coach.

With a very calm, understanding tone, his father replied, "It's no big deal, every team has a player on it who sucks."

Bruce couldn't believe what he just heard. Such words of wisdom! Are you kidding? It's great to be honest with your kids, but was it necessary to be quite *that* brutally honest? Without using these exact words, he told his son, "Yes, it's true, you really do suck at baseball, and the kids who are ridiculing you are 100 percent right!"

Where's Ward Cleaver when you need him? I think this dad needed a consultation with Ward before talking to his son. Ward always knew just what to say to comfort his troubled son, unlike this guy!

Bruce ran away in horror after what he heard, completely forgetting about the lost bat. The ten-year-old baseball hater stopped playing baseball shortly after that great talk with his dad/coach. Why did he quit playing? He thought baseball wasn't fun. What a surprise!

"YOU GUYS BLEW THAT CALL, AND I'VE GOT VIDEO EVIDENCE!"

While I was umpiring a fifteen-year-old Babe Ruth game, one of the parents had a very impressive-looking camera and shot pictures and videos during the entire game. Halfway through the game, a batter scorched a ground ball to the right of the shortstop who dove to make a great backhanded stab. He jumped up, whirled, and fired a bullet to the first baseman who made an outstanding stretch while keeping his foot on the bag. The batter was hustling, the throw was on target, and this play was as close as it gets.

As the plate umpire, my job was to make sure the first baseman kept his foot on the base while stretching to catch the throw and be ready to help if the base umpire needed it. From what I saw, the throw arrived a nanosecond before the batter's foot came down on the base. The base umpire made a loud and decisive "HE'S OUT!" call. I gave the base umpire a nod, telling him silently "good call." The crowd was buzzing, as it was a great fielding play by the shortstop and a great stretch by the first baseman.

Suddenly, the lady with the camera came running onto the field yelling, "Time out, time out! He was safe, you guys totally blew that call and I've got video evidence to prove it!"

Shaking our heads, the other umpire and I call "time," and the coaches of the photographer's team and the other team's coaches all come onto the field to join the party.

"Ma'am," I said, "parents can't call time and come running onto the field. Can you please leave the field so we can continue the game?"

"But he was safe," she said emphatically, "and I can show that you guys blew the call if you look at the evidence."

This was getting comical. "Look, I'm sorry," I said, "but we don't use video replay, whether the call was right or wrong."

Her team's coach said, "Sally, he's right, let it go."

"Okay," she said, and left the field.

After the inning was over, I said to the photographer, "Hey, when the game is over, I'd like to take a look, because I'm pretty sure we got the call right."

After the game, she showed me the evidence, which was even better than a video. Her camera was set on "continuous shooting mode," producing multiple pictures per second while the batter was running to first base. I really couldn't tell anything by looking into the camera and asked if she could email the footage to me so I could see a much larger picture on a computer screen.

When I saw the pictures on my computer that night, they were much clearer, and it was incredible just how close this play was. I saw a tiny white blur, which was the ball, in the mesh of the pocket of the first baseman's glove as the batter's front foot was four inches above and about to come down on first base. She insisted the batter was safe because the ball was hard to see, but I saw it in the glove of the first baseman. Great call by the base ump!

As for video replay, I wish youth baseball had it. I'd love

to see whether I get close calls right or not. Since replay started, those heated arguments in big league games with umpires and managers screaming at each other, faces one inch apart, that were so entertaining are now history. In the pros, if a manager disagrees with a call, it goes to replay, and whatever the decision is, that's the end of it. I'd love to have that luxury as well, if for no other reason than to stop coaches from "appealing" every close call on the bases that goes against them—which they aren't allowed to do but do it constantly anyway.

DO YOU KNOW WHAT THIS MEANS? NOW WE HAVE TO KEEP PLAYING!

Some youth baseball games are poorly played and move so slowly it seems like they go on for days. Parents watching are so bored they just want the agony to be over. In a 2021 classic yawner I was umpiring, with two outs in the bottom of the fourth inning, the visiting team held a ten-run lead. Everyone watching held their breath, praying to the baseball gods for the home team to make the final out, so the game would end after four innings (instead of six) because of the ten-run mercy rule.

With a runner on second, the batter singled into center field. The third base coach waved on the runner to try to score. The center fielder made a great throw, but the runner slid in easily, way ahead of the tag. The play wasn't close at all.

No comments from players or coaches, but I heard a parent loud and clear, sitting behind the backstop shout in disgust, "Oh, come on ump, he was out by a mile!"

I was a bit mystified by this comment because the runner slid in at least two seconds before the ball even reached the catcher. Then I heard two other parents laughing, and one of them blurted out, "You guys know what this means? Now they're only up by nine, so we gotta keep playing! If he was out, the game would've ended! I'm taking a nap. Wake me when it's over."

I don't know if these parents were on the winning side or the losing side, but it was a pretty funny comment that summed up how everyone watching this game felt. Everybody just wanted the boredom to end, including me!

"ARE YOU CALLING US CHEATERS?"

Sometimes rival teams in competitive leagues, for whatever reason, just don't like each other. In many of these situations, the obnoxious parents on opposing sides are much more of a problem than the players or coaches. I was umpiring a double header of fourteen-year-olds in July of 2019 on a day that was way too hot to be playing one baseball game, never mind two.

The temperature was pushing one hundred degrees, with humidity off the charts. There were heat stroke advisory warnings and everyone was told to stay out of the sun. Of course, we had two games to play, and the show must go on!

The sun was pounding down on the field with no shade anywhere. My umpiring partner and I were drowning in sweat after the first inning of game one. We'd been warned these rival teams had some problems in the past. A few chippy comments went back and forth but nothing major happened in the first game. It was ridiculously hot, and by game two the heat was getting to people.

In the third inning of game two, with the score tied and a runner on first, the visiting team crushed a triple to deep center field that absolutely exploded off the bat, scoring the go-ahead run from first. Calls of "BLUE, TIME! HE USED AN ILLEGAL BAT!" rang out from the home team bench.

Out comes the list of bats that are approved and not approved. The bat was illegal, so we took appropriate action. The batter who hit the triple was called out, the run scored was taken off the board, and the illegal bat was taken out of the game. It was all handled smoothly, the guilty team's manager apologized, no players said anything, and everyone was ready to move on. End of story, right?

No, sir, no how, no way, not in my games! That would be way too easy. Who would want that?

Since players and coaches all handled the situation calmly, parents had to step in and "SCREW IT UP." How could parents screw this up? As mentioned earlier, parents have an easy job. All they have to do is just sit and watch the game. Apparently, that job is much harder than it seems. Since players and coaches were behaving, let's find some obnoxious parents to get everybody all riled up!

One parent (let's call him Genius #1) yelled to his rival parents, "Yeah, that's the only way you guys can beat us, by using illegal bats. You're a bunch of cheaters!"

Another parent, an even bigger genius (let's call him Genius #2) on the other side yelled back, "Oh, yeah? Are you calling us cheaters? He's used that bat all season, so why is it suddenly illegal?"

When I heard what Genius #2 said, in my opinion as an impartial observer, since his team *was* using an illegal bat—apparently all season—this was an utterly pathetic comeback by Genius #2. Genius #1, like a great white shark smelling blood in the water, went in for the kill.

Genius #1 screamed back, "You're not only cheaters, you're also idiots! The bat's always been illegal, this is just the first time you got caught!"

Outstanding comeback by Genius #1! This devastating

blow staggered Genius #2, reminding me of the vicious uppercut from a young George Foreman in 1973 that dropped reigning heavyweight boxing champion Joe Frazier to the canvas, prompting the late Howard Cosell's legendary call of "DOWN GOES FRAZIER! DOWN GOES FRAZIER!"

I'm certain I heard the voice of Howard Cosell screaming from the heavens, "DOWN GOES GENIUS #2!, DOWN GOES GENIUS #2!"

While I agreed with Genius #1 about their opponents both cheating AND being idiots, tempers were flaring, and this was rapidly getting out of control. Genius #2 and the visiting team's parents were writhing in agony following the brutal tongue-lashing of Genius #1. It was ninety-nine degrees out, the argument was escalating, angry parents on the opposing sides were moving toward each other, so the other umpire and I stepped in before this became a full-fledged brawl.

"Okay, everybody, sit down, calm down, take a breath, not another word about this from anybody, or the game ends right now in a forfeit for both teams!"

Nobody wanted that, they were all having so much fun!

Umpires only threaten to do that as a last resort, and fortunately, it worked. All the angry geniuses calmed down, no punches were thrown, no shots were fired, and peace was restored throughout the land. Genius #1, Genius #2, and all the obnoxious parents somehow avoided killing each other during the Great Sweat Fest of 2019.

"OFFICER, COULD YOU PLEASE WALK ME TO MY CAR?"

Tensions can run high in summer all-star travel team games, especially in the playoffs. A town's best eight-through-twelve-year-old teams compete with all-star players of the same age from other towns. These games are very competitive compared to spring recreational games. They play to win. In other words, everyone's out for blood!

I was the plate umpire for a semifinal game of the eleven-year-old group. In this matchup, the visiting team's parents had a reputation for riding the umpires and lived up to their reputation. On every ball, strike, safe, or out call, complaints from these parents were nonstop.

In what was expected to be a very close game, the visitors scored early and often, and led by ten runs after batting in the top of the fourth inning. If the home team couldn't score in the bottom of the fourth, the game would end by the ten-run mercy rule. The home team stayed alive with one run on a close play at the plate that the visiting parents all screamed about. Four big guys who all looked like lumberjacks were the instigators, leading the nonstop barrage of abuse by the visiting parents against the umpires. They stood against the fence behind third base the entire game, with their arms crossed. I affectionately referred to them as the "angry mob."

After the fourth inning, they were really letting us have it, "You know this game should be over—he was out at the plate by a mile."

I walked over to the angry mob and said, "Hey, guys, c'mon, you're up by nine runs with two innings left."

One of them fired back at me, "We'd be out of here by now if you hadn't blown that call."

I fired back, "Knock it off, or YOU will be out of here!"

I spotted, on the home team bleachers, the mom of one of the players. She was a police officer in her full police uniform—gun and everything—watching the game. I asked her, "Hey, will you be here for the rest of the game?"

"Of course, why?" she asked.

"I think this could get ugly, and I might need backup!" I replied. She and other home team parents had been hearing how much grief the umpires were getting from the visiting parents.

"I'll be here," she assured me.

"Thanks, officer!" I said, as we were about to start inning number five. The home team trailed by nine runs, and for four innings couldn't do anything. The visitors were held scoreless in the top of the fifth. In the bottom of the fifth, the home team figured it out, mounted a furious comeback, and the visitors, who'd been in complete control, suddenly couldn't get out of their own way. Helped by walks, dropped fly balls, booted grounders, and bad pitching, the home team scored eight runs, cutting the deficit to one.

The visitors again couldn't score in the top of the sixth. The "angry mob" yelled and screamed incessantly. I asked the visiting manager to speak to them, which he did. The coaches and players all behaved perfectly the whole game, so again, here come the parents to "screw it up"!

In the bottom of the sixth and final inning, the drama was nonstop after the first two batters were quickly retired on popups. With the game on the line, the next two batters singled, and the following batter drew a walk. With two outs and bases loaded, a routine grounder to the second baseman should have ended the game, but he booted the grounder, then made a bad throw to first, which beat the runner, but the first baseman pulled his foot off the bag stretching to catch the low throw. SAFE AT FIRST! The runner that was on third base crossed the plate. TIE GAME!

The call at first base was correct, but not according to "the angry mob." The loss of a ten-run lead, according to them, was all because of the umpires. Bases were still loaded, and the first pitch to the next batter was way inside, hitting the batter and driving in the winning run!

"ARE YOU BLIND?" screamed the ringleader of the angry mob. "HE MADE NO EFFORT TO GET OUT OF THE WAY OF THE PITCH!"

Their team blew a ten-run lead, lost the game, and in their minds, it was entirely the fault of the umpires. Booted grounders, bad throws, dropped fly balls, inability to throw strikes—none of that had caused the loss. It was all on the umpires. Even the last batter getting hit by the pitch was because of the umpires. One yelled that I was "blind as a bat," and the base umpire took his share of abuse as well. We turned a deaf ear and just wanted to get out of there. The base umpire, who was sixteen, got picked up by his parents so, fortunately, he was gone quickly.

I noticed the "angry mob" had shifted their location to an area between where I was and the parking lot, so now I'd have to walk right by them to get to my car. They stood with their arms crossed, glaring at me the entire time. I killed some time talking with parents for a few minutes, hoping the "angry mob" would disperse, but they weren't moving. I just wanted to leave without dealing with these clowns, who were clearly waiting for me, no doubt wanting to have a "discussion" with me!

There were four of them, and one of me. These guys were all twice my size, half my age, and not happy. I had no intention of going anywhere near them.

Suddenly, I had an idea. The police officer was still there. I wanted to ask if I could borrow her gun for a few minutes but doubted she'd agree to that. Instead, I asked, "Officer, can you do me a favor? Could you please walk me to my car? Those four guys are definitely standing there waiting for me."

"Sure, no problem," she said. "I can't believe how crazy some parents get over an eleven-year-old's baseball game."

"Thanks, I really appreciate your help," I said. "I don't need a confrontation with these idiots, I just want to go home."

As we walked right by them, they turned away pretending they didn't notice us. Nobody said anything. She stayed by my car while I got my umpire gear off, with the "angry mob" still there, glaring at me, arms still crossed fifty feet away. I got in the car and thanked her for helping me out. She walked back to the field, and I started to drive away.

But the "angry mob" wasn't done. They had one more thing to say to me, but this time they used "sign language" instead of words. As I drove toward them, they continued to glare at me. When I passed by them, simultaneously all four of them gave me "the finger."

Classy move, guys! Their in-game behavior was pathetic, but their goodbye to me was over the line. I contacted the home team league president, who reported the incident and the behavior of the visiting team parents to both the board of the visiting team and the board of the summer travel league.

The emails started to fly the next day. The summer travel league board issued a stern warning to the visiting team's board that they'd be banned from the summer travel league if anything like this ever happened again. The visiting team's board responded with not only an apology to the summer league board, but apologies to me and the other umpire.

A few days later, I received the "icing on the cake." The other umpire and I both received, in the mail (not email), a letter written and signed by all twenty-four parents of the visiting team's players apologizing for their "unacceptable behavior," along with assurances that nothing like this would ever happen again. It was quite comical, and I pull it out every now and then when I need a good laugh.

This letter reminded me of being back in grade school when the teacher would make some jerk who was always annoying another student stay after school and write on the blackboard fifty times, "I will not pull Suzy Martin's ponytails ever again."

You wouldn't think police protection for umpires is necessary at youth baseball games, and usually, it isn't. After that episode, however, when I'm umpiring, I'm always thrilled to see a uniformed officer in the crowd. You just never know when an "angry mob" might appear. THANKS AGAIN, OFFICER!

DEALING WITH CELEBRITY PARENTS

Umpires sometimes work youth baseball games where former professional athletes are either watching their son's game or even coaching their team. Some are nice, some are jerks, and some, just like "regular people," are obnoxious parents who take youth baseball games way too seriously. You'd think that a wealthy, former professional athlete would know better than to give an umpire—who's lucky if he's making fifty bucks—grief during a youth baseball game, but it happens. Here are a few stories of umpires dealing with well-known former pro athletes.

THE FIRST FORMER PRO ATHLETE THAT REALLY SHOULD KNOW BETTER

(Contributed by Rick from Rhode Island)

In 2012, Rick, an umpire from Rhode Island, got a call from an umpire assignor for youth games in a nearby town. He asked Rick to do him a favor and umpire a game of eight-year-olds. Normally, teenage umpires handle these games.

One of these teams had a parent who was out of control at his eight-year-old son's games. He'd stand behind the backstop, and when he disagreed with calls made by youth umpires, he let them know about it, intimidating the umpires and opposing players. He'd shout instructions constantly to his son and the players on his son's team, even though he wasn't a coach.

The league asked if an adult could umpire a game and deal with this unruly parent if necessary. These games are usually officiated by thirteen- or fourteen-year-old youth umpires, as state-certified, commonly known as "patched," umpires like Rick are unnecessary for these games. The players are very young and just learning the game. Pitchers can barely reach the plate, never mind throw strikes. These games seem to go on for days and are often "walk-a-thons."

After agreeing to work the game, the assignor told Rick

the name of the parent, who was a very well-known former professional athlete. Rick thought from radio or TV interviews that he seemed like a nice guy, but apparently, he was just another obnoxious parent who took his son's baseball games way too seriously.

Rick was ready to put this guy in his place. You'd think a former professional athlete would know better. The coaches were surprised when Rick showed up to umpire the game instead of a youth umpire. He explained why he was there and was prepared to handle the problem-parent if he didn't behave.

As the game started, Rick saw the parent in question standing behind the bench of his son's team. He stayed there the entire game, never once going behind the backstop. He clapped and cheered for his son and his team. In between innings, he helped the catcher get his equipment on. He was encouraging and positive, everything that you could possibly ask of a parent watching an eight-year-old's baseball game. He was "doing his job," NOT screwing it up, like Rick expected him to.

The game was terrible, as Rick anticipated, a typical "comedy of errors" game. Not one negative word was heard from this parent about balls or strikes, even though Rick's strike zone was so big you could drive a truck through it!

Rick wondered if he was in the right place, as he came prepared for battle, and nothing except positive words were heard from the former pro athlete. After the game ended, Rick was in the parking lot taking his umpire gear off, and a big black SUV with tinted windows rolled slowly by. The driver's window went down, and the formerly obnoxious–now model parent said to Rick, with a big smile, "Hey, Blue, thanks! You did a great job today!" and drove off into the sunset.

As an umpire, you never know what to expect in games, and sometimes when you're ready for anything, you get nothing!

"YOU CAN'T EJECT ME. DON'T YOU KNOW WHO I AM?" (THE SECOND FORMER PRO ATHLETE THAT REALLY SHOULD KNOW BETTER)

(Contributed by Malcolm from Missouri)

Malcolm shared with me a story of a very well-known retired big-league pitcher who was a coach for his eight-year-old son's team in Missouri in 1999. Malcolm, now a veteran umpire in his thirties, was only fifteen at the time, and umpiring a game of seven- and eight-year-olds. As expected, the pitching was horrible, and like the previous story, the strike zone had to be "generous."

Throughout the game, this coach commented quietly about Malcolm's strike zone. As the game went on, the comments got louder, more frequent, and became more like arguments than comments. In the third inning, Malcolm said politely to the coach, "Sir, please stop making comments about balls and strikes."

He continued his commentary. In the fourth inning, Malcolm said, "Coach, I asked you before to please stop, and if you continue to argue balls and strikes, I will have no choice but to eject you from the game."

The coach rolled his eyes and kept quiet until the next inning, when the comments started again, getting even louder and more frequent. Malcolm had heard enough.

"Coach, I'm sorry, but I've warned you twice about arguing balls and strikes. I'm ejecting you from the game. Please leave the field."

"WHAT?" said the coach, looking completely bewildered. "You can't eject me. DON'T YOU KNOW WHO I AM?"

"Yes, Mr. _____, I know who you are, and you of all people should know that you can't argue balls and strikes, even for kids this age."

So, the rich and famous former big-leaguer was ejected from coaching a seven- and eight-year-old's game for arguing balls and strikes with a fifteen-year-old umpire. Well done, Malcolm!

THE VERY CHATTY FORMER PRO ATHLETE

No problems here. This is a "nice tale" of a very pleasant encounter I had with a well-known former Boston athlete. As I made my way onto the field before umpiring a fourteen-year-old Babe Ruth game, I walked by parents seated outside the fence on the home team side. Some said the usual, "Hi, Blue, how ya' doin'?" I passed another parent seated off by himself with his face down looking at his phone who piped up jokingly, "Hey, Blue, my son's number seven. Take good care of him!"

I wouldn't have even recognized him if he hadn't said anything. He'd put on a few pounds since his playing days ended, was wearing a hat, and was looking down at his phone. But as soon as he spoke, I instantly recognized the voice of a star of Boston's 2004 baseball team that won their first title in eighty-six years. Other umpires who'd worked games with him watching all said he sits by himself, never speaks to anyone, and seemed to like being left alone.

Maybe it's my charming personality, or I was just lucky, but this former player that everyone said "liked to be left alone" initiated the conversation with me and was really in the mood to talk that day.

We briefly chatted a few times between innings. I mentioned to him that, in 2004, his first year with the team, I took my son to his first game at Fenway Park, and he was my son's favorite player. I gave him a good laugh telling him that when the team won the championship later that year for the first time since 1918, my son, who was only eight at the time, excitedly proclaimed, "DAD, I'VE WAITED MY WHOLE LIFE FOR THIS!"

When the game ended, I was leaving the field. He called out to me, tossed me a ball, and said, "Hey, Blue, give this to your son."

It was an autographed baseball that I didn't even ask for!

Thanks for the souvenir, and thanks even more for helping our guys finally get the job done so the last conversation I could have with my eighty-year-old dad before he passed away less than two weeks after Boston won the championship was about how happy he was to have lived long enough to finally see Boston win it all. But what made this magical playoff run so sweet for older fans like my dad wasn't even the final series where Boston swept St. Louis in four straight games. In the prior series against the team from the Bronx that Bostonians are all trained from birth to despise, the good guys lost the first three games of the best of seven series. Facing elimination, these loveable players who nicknamed themselves "a bunch of idiots" became the first team in big-league baseball history to win a seven-game series after dropping the first three. To witness this feat was incredible, but to have taken down our dreaded archrivals from New York in the process was, for fans from Boston, as good as it gets in sports. THANKS AGAIN!

TALES OF RUTHLESS COACHES

WHY IS WINNING YOUTH BASEBALL GAMES SO DAMN IMPORTANT?

I've never understood why it's so important to win when you coach, especially in a recreational league where the emphasis is not supposed to be on winning. It's certainly more fun to win than lose at anything, but why does it matter so much?

For a trophy and bragging rights? Who cares? Other than making you proud, what does winning really do for the middle-aged youth baseball coach?

Winning youth baseball games WILL NOT change your life. Your real job won't suck any less. Your net worth will not increase. Winning won't make you younger, reverse receding hairlines, or transform flabby midsections into a set of rock-hard, six-pack abs.

When I coached, I never noticed that my wife found me more attractive on nights after my team of nine-year-olds won than after we lost. Did she? Maybe she did. I don't know. I'll have to ask her sometime.

NOT ALL COACHES ARE LIKE ME

I incorrectly assumed when I began coaching that all coaches in recreational leagues operated similarly to me. Players are rotated defensively in and out the entire game. Since only nine played defensively at the same time, one or more players had to sit out defensively each inning. I had a very simple formula depending on how many players I had for a game:

With ten players: six of the ten sit one inning each.

With eleven players: ten sit one inning, one sits out two innings.

With twelve players: all twelve sit two innings each.

I made sure every player played at least one inning in the infield and one inning in the outfield. All players batted in a "continuous batting order," even if sitting out defensively. I'd change the batting order each game, rather than always hit the best batter first and the worst always last as most coaches did. Sometimes, I'd let whoever got to the field first write their name anywhere they wanted on the batting order sheet. Trust me, that got them to the field early! Sometimes the players picked names out of a hat to determine the batting order. I'd try anything to make it fun, especially for players that were not stars.

MAKING THE GAME FUN BY AWARDING A "GAME BALL"

As a manager, after every game, whether we won or lost, I'd award one of my players the "game ball." I'd take a beaten-up baseball from the game, carefully inscribe it with the player's name, the words "GAME BALL," the date of the game, and a short description of what earned them this coveted honor.

I see from time-to-time kids I coached fifteen years ago. Now in their mid–late twenties, they've tossed all their dust-collecting trophies, but still have these priceless "game ball" treasures. We'd usually have eleven or twelve players on the team and play about twenty games. On most teams, there were one or two players who were the stars, so the challenge was to get less talented players a "game ball" and not just give it to the stars every game.

My rule was that everybody on the team would get a "game ball" at least once, and nobody could earn a second until everyone got their first. At times, I dreamed up ways to get horrible players a "game ball." Once, I gave a "game ball" to our worst hitter who was hit by a pitch with the bases loaded to drive in a run. Creative things like that! Everyone loved it, and better players knew exactly what I was doing when I'd concoct some clever way to give a "game ball" to weaker players.

It was a FUN moment after every game, whether we won or lost, as everyone on the team eagerly awaited my announcement of who earned the "game ball." Remember, BASEBALL IS SUPPOSED TO BE FUN!

COACHES AREN'T ALWAYS FAIR ABOUT PLAYING TIME

Since players at the top of the lineup often bat one more time than those at the bottom, it makes sense to switch the lineup around from game to game. While this is fair to all players, it won't give you the strongest possible lineup.

League rules stated everyone must play at least three innings defensively and one inning must be an infield position. There were no rules about batting order, or about all players sitting out equal amounts when there were ten, eleven, or twelve players. No rule stated that everyone must play in the outfield.

So, to comply with the rules, even though I don't think it's fair to all players in a recreational league, what coaches who need to "win at all costs" do is:

- **Batting:** Best hitter bats first, worst hitter bats last, always, every game, never a change.
- **Defensively:** Best players never play the outfield, and never sit out a single inning. They play every inning as pitcher, catcher, first base, second base, or shortstop. Weaker defensive players sit on the bench for three innings, then play two innings buried in the

outfield, then one mandatory inning in the infield, usually third base, and the coach prays nothing gets hit their way.

I had problems with this mind-set because BASEBALL IS SUPPOSED TO BE FUN!

1. Baseball isn't fun when you sit out half the game, watching others play the whole game.
2. Baseball isn't fun when you always bat last. You might as well walk around wearing a sign around your neck that says, "Hey, everybody, look at me, I'm the worst batter on my team!"
3. For weaker defensive players, they don't develop infield skills because they're usually buried in right field. Also, not fun.
4. For stronger defensive players, when they make the all-star travel team and must play outfield, they have no outfield skills because they've never played there before.
5. Making all players play and sit out an equal number of innings and requiring all players to play both infield and outfield positions each game makes sense. It gives everyone equal playing time and lessens the chance stars will dominate games.

Unfortunately, when a coach like me goes against a coach who does whatever it takes to win, it's me who loses, but that's not important. The ones who really lose are the kids who just want to have fun playing baseball but sit on the bench for half the game. SITTING ON THE BENCH ISN'T FUN!

COACHES DREAMING UP "OUTSIDE THE BOX" MOTIVATIONAL TECHNIQUES

Some parents of players are also managers or assistant coaches. Most played baseball as kids and wanted to spend time teaching their sons to play. Though not trained coaches, most know enough to teach kids the basics.

While trying to find ways to lead their troops to the top of the standings, some coaches came up with bizarre ways to try to reach their goals. While it's good to think "outside of the box," some of these coaches were just out of their minds. Here's a few tales of overly competitive coaches trying strange ways to be great motivators to win games, because that was all they cared about.

"I'LL OFFER A TWENTY-DOLLAR REWARD FOR ANYONE WHO CAN..."

(Contributed by Billy in Iowa)

In 2019, one of Billy's fellow coaches in his Iowa recreational league had played college ball and was very knowledgeable. Coach Jack was a good coach but was one of those guys that NEVER STOPS TALKING! Jack had a big, booming voice you could hear a mile away. He tried to be a great motivator, giving loud, high-energy speeches before games that would've made Knute Rockne proud.

"C'mon, boys, show me desire, I want energy! Take that extra base, dive for that ball, dig deep, and fire that pitch even when you've got nothing left! Give it everything you've got! Do it for the team—T-E-A-M, team, team, team! Show me how much you want it, boys, now let's go and do it!"

And that was only the pre-game speech. He was just getting started. All game long, Jack shouted instructions to all nine players on the field. "Infielders, down and ready; outfielders on your toes. Willy, make those pitches, hit your spots, show me you want it more than they do. James, a couple steps in and three to your left. Timmy, five steps back and four to your right. Benny, close to the bag at third, stay low and ready, nothing gets by you."

Same deal with batters. "Lucas, eyes on the ball, step toward the pitcher, start your swing early, watch the pitcher, attack the good ones, lay off high ones. Open your stance, close your stance, keep your weight back, move back in the box, move up in the box, elbow up, bend your knees, toes in, choke up, head still," and on and on. No wonder Lucas swung and missed. He forgot the first instruction, to "keep your eyes on the ball," while trying to remember the other forty-seven instructions he was subsequently given.

Baserunners also got a barrage of instructions: "Runners, moving on contact, slide on close plays. Mikey, you're scoring on anything to the right side. Billy, don't get doubled up, Bobby, don't get picked off."

On and on Coach Jack talked, and when will he stop? NEVER!

In one of Billy's games against Jack's team, the mom of one of his players was overheard saying to another parent, "God, this guy's giving me a headache! I'll offer a twenty-dollar cash reward right here, right now, to anyone who can get him to shut the f--k up for just two minutes! Please, just two minutes of silence, that's all I ask!"

REWARD THEM WHEN THEY WIN, AND PUNISH THEM WHEN THEY LOSE

(Contributed by Glen from Indiana)

In 2015, Glen umpired for a recreational league in Indiana. One of the managers, Coach Forrest, was super nice to his players, but only if they won. When they'd win a game, he'd pick up the tab for every player on his team to buy an ice cream from the truck that was always at the baseball field at the end of games. Other times, he'd have the local pizza shop deliver pizza for everybody—but only if they won the game.

Glen noticed that whenever the team didn't win, there was no pizza or ice cream for the players. Instead, the whole team ran laps around the perimeter of the field. The number of runs the team lost by were the number of laps they had to run. If they lost by two runs, they ran two laps. If they lost by five runs, five laps. When they lost by eight or nine runs, they were doing laps for a while.

Just to show he was a nice guy, if it was only one lap, Coach Forrest would run the lap with his players. On more than one occasion, this sight prompted any remaining spectators to begin chanting in unison these words from the 1994 movie, *Forrest Gump*:

"RUN, FORREST, RUN!"

MOTIVATION BY HUMILIATION

(Contributed by Kelvin in Minnesota)

In 2017, Mac was another manager in Kelvin's Minnesota recreational league. Although everyone liked him as a person, Mac was consumed with winning. If the team won, he was nice to his players. When they lost, he'd tell them how lousy they played.

One week, Mac dreamed up a new way to motivate his players after a bad game to play better. In a Monday game, one of his players had a terrible game. Peter was awful, both offensively and defensively, and the team lost. During this game, he dropped an easy flyball and made a wild throw, which both sent in extra runs. He struck out twice with the bases loaded to kill rallies.

After the game, Mac spoke to the team, saying that, starting now, whenever anybody has a really bad game, they'll have to turn in their team shirt for the night. He asked Peter to give him his shirt and said he could have it back the next day. Peter complied but wasn't happy. He felt bad enough that he had a terrible game. Now his coach was humiliating him in front of the whole team!

On Wednesday, Mac's team lost again. This time he made two players, Tony and Danny, give back their shirts. The players clearly didn't like this, and rather than motivating anyone, it seemed to make everyone afraid they'd have a bad game and be the next player to lose their shirt for the night.

On Saturday morning, the team played even worse, losing badly to a team they should have easily beaten. This time instead of singling anyone out, Mac took a team approach, telling his players, "On your way out of the dugout, I want everyone to give me back your shirts!"

One by one, the players filed out with their heads down, some almost in tears, and gave Coach Mac their team shirts.

The players left and Coach Mac drove home. The minute he arrived, his phone started ringing, and it was an angry parent. A minute later, another angry parent. As soon as he hung up, the phone rang again and a third parent voiced their displeasure with Mac making his son give his team shirt back. By now, Mac was beginning to think this motivational ploy might not have been such a great idea.

The phone rang again, and this time it was the league president, who told Mac he'd just gotten four calls from parents furious about Mac making kids turn in their shirts because they lost the game. "They aren't serious, are they? Please tell me you didn't really do this," he pleaded with Mac.

When Mac confessed, the head of the league strongly suggested that Mac take an immediate "road trip." Coach Mac took his advice. After apologizing first to his own son, he spent the next three hours driving around town, ringing doorbells, returning shirts, and apologizing to his players and their parents. Nice way to spend a Saturday afternoon!

I thought Jack's motivational speeches were a bit much, Forrest making players run laps whenever they lost was crazy, and Mac will never be hired as a motivational consultant. None of these brilliant ideas worked!

"LET'S ALL COACH TOGETHER AND OUR TEAM WILL DESTROY EVERYBODY!"

(Contributed by Paul in Arizona)

In their quest to sidestep the normal way teams were assembled, three clever dads in Arizona found a way, in 2010, to gain a clear-cut advantage over every other team.

At the time, the league that Paul coached in allowed a manager to select his two assistant coaches before drafting players, and their sons would automatically play together on the same team. It was intended as a way that if two or three dads were friends, they'd coach together and their kids, who were also friends, could be on the same team. It seemed harmless in a recreational league, having two or three friends coaching the same team together. It wasn't a problem, until one year, when three dads who barely knew each other, had a brilliant idea.

These dads had sons who were the best players in the league. One said to the others, "If I manage the team, and you two are my assistant coaches, with our three kids playing together, we'll never lose a game!"

And they didn't. They rolled through the nine- and ten-year-old league demolishing every team in their path. They finished the season with a perfect record of twenty wins and no losses and having the three best pitchers and hitters in the league certainly helped. Paul, and every other coach, questioned why they even bothered playing games that season. With the three best players on the same team, the championship trophy for that season should have been handed to these ingenious dads before the first pitch was ever thrown.

After countless complaints all season, the league rules were amended so that in future years, managers could no longer select their assistant coaches first to build a "super team." Instead, managers had to select their players through a draft process, and then select assistant coaches from the parents of players they drafted. The draft process, which will be detailed shortly, in some leagues is so complex, it borders on absurdity. It does, however, prevent coaches who'd do "whatever it takes to win" from using this method to build a team stacked with the best players. They'd need to be even more creative in the future.

ANOTHER WAY TO "STACK A TEAM": JUST DO IT YOURSELF

(Contributed by Ben from Pennsylvania)

An old expression says, "If you want something done right, just do it yourself." Most youth leagues hold some type of draft to place players on teams. The intention is to have equally balanced teams so that one team doesn't win every game while another loses every game. The draft process, which I'll describe shortly, is a lengthy, complicated, time-consuming endeavor that ties up a bunch of people for hours.

In 2012, in the Arizona league where Ben coached, a crafty veteran manager offered to put together the teams himself for his spring rec league, eliminating the need that year to hold a draft. Very nice of him—except for an ulterior motive, which nobody realized until the season began. After a couple of games, it was apparent to everyone that the ten best players in the eighty-player league were all on his team. Like the three clever dads, this manager's team also crushed everybody, going undefeated, and winning the championship.

When questioned, he pleaded ignorance, claiming he had no idea how good some of the players on his team were. The only benefit to this was when the time came to assemble an all-star summer travel team, it was already done. No need for tryouts. The summer all-star travel team was his regular spring-season team!

FINDING A LOOPHOLE IN THE RULES

(Contributed by Andrew in Colorado)

"A long time ago in a galaxy far, far away," a baseball game took place between two teams of nine- and ten-year-olds. Actually, the game was played in 1999 in Colorado, not that long ago, and not in another galaxy, but I've always liked that *Star Wars* intro and wanted to use it somewhere.

In a close game, Coach Andrew reported that Coach Jimmy found a gray area or a "loophole" in their league rules about how pitchers could be used, which he utilized to win the game. After Jimmy's ace pitcher started the game, pitching three no-hit innings, he was taken out and replaced with another pitcher. After five innings, Jimmy's team led by one run. In the top of the sixth inning, Andrew's team's last chance, his players noticed that the starting pitcher, who was replaced after three innings, came back in as the pitcher to finish the game.

It's common knowledge among players and coaches that once a pitcher is taken out and replaced with another pitcher, he can still play other positions, but can't pitch again in the same game, so Andrew approached Jimmy, and this was their conversation:

Andrew said, "Hey, what's Paul [the ace pitcher] doing

back on the mound? He already pitched and you replaced him, so he can't pitch again in this game."

Jimmy said, "Where does it say in our rules that I can't pitch him again?"

Andrew replied, "C'mon, man, it might not actually say it in our rules, but everybody knows you can't do that!"

"Show me in the rules where it says I can't! I have the rules right here, and I am quoting rule number one, which states that free substitution is allowed throughout the game!"

Jimmy was ready for the objection. He showed Andrew the official rule sheet, which just happened to be in his shirt pocket. Even though nobody ever used this tactic, it wasn't specifically stated anywhere in the league rules that it couldn't be done. Jimmy refused to give in, put his starting pitcher back in for the final inning, and three quick outs ended the game.

Andrew had to give the man credit. Jimmy had done his homework, analyzing the exact wording of the rule. The way the rule was written, Jimmy was 100 percent correct and had done nothing wrong. Unfortunately, Andrew's players didn't agree. They thought Coach Jimmy cheated. Andrew's players were upset, not because they lost a close game, but because they lost to a team that didn't play by the rules.

One of his players said to Andrew after the game, "Coach, you know what I learned from this game?"

"What did you learn today?" Andrew asked his nine-year-old player. "That sometimes, no matter how hard you try, the other team might be just a little bit better?"

"Oh, no, coach, everybody knows that. What I learned today is that it's okay to cheat to win as long you can get away with it." When the player said this, the rest of the team all nodded their heads in agreement.

Andrew was stunned by what this nine-year-old had just said, as any sensible coach would be. Losing the game didn't matter to Andrew, but he was very concerned about what his players learned from this game.

The next day, after Andrew told the league's commissioner what happened, rule number one was amended to clearly state, "Free substitution is allowed throughout the game, with the exception of a pitcher who, once removed as pitcher, can continue to play in the game in any other defensive position, but cannot pitch again in the same game."

Stuff like this has always driven me crazy. Some coaches need to win so badly that they try to be smarter than everyone else. Pushing the boundaries of a gray area, finding a loophole, and BENDING a rule, even if you aren't technically breaking one, is not sending the right message to players. As parents and coaches, we have a responsibility to teach children and players right from wrong, not how to bend or break rules and get away with it.

For some coaches, winning becomes an addiction. Once they experience winning, even in a youth recreational league, they get seduced and become hopelessly infatuated by the evil temptress known as "Victory." Once they've savored the sweet taste of victory, they want more of it and will do anything to get it. They forget why they decided to coach their child's team in the first place because winning is what they think about and all that matters to them.

It's almost like watching a really bad, low-budget horror movie when a good person's mind, body, and soul are taken over and possessed by evil demons. Without even realizing it, another coach becomes "one of them," a ruthless coach who is totally obsessed with winning.

"WE'LL BE WATCHING YOU"

If impressionable young children who play youth sports could send a message to parents and coaches about how they soak up everything they see and hear from adults, those four words say it all. Every disrespectful, inappropriate word grown-ups say and every sneaky, devious move they make—nothing goes unnoticed.

Coaches and parents of impressionable young kids are role models. Ultra-competitive coaches and parents must be careful what they say and do. Kids hear everything they say, watch everything they do, learn from them, and behave like them. Kids miss nothing! A coach is like a parent to every member of their team during the time they spend together.

When kids see adults act inappropriately, they assume it's okay to do similar things themselves.

In the previous story, a nine-year-old said he learned that "it's okay to cheat to win as long as you can get away with it." While I'm sure this coach had absolutely no intention of teaching kids this, that's exactly what the actions he took to satisfy his overwhelming need to win did. What kids learn from adults on the field or court becomes how they will handle competitive or difficult situations, both in sports and in life.

Grown-ups need to teach kids right from wrong, not how

to do what's wrong and get away with it. Young kids don't need to be shown how to be sneaky, devious, and underhanded. They'll have plenty of time when they're older to learn that stuff on their own!

COUNTING PITCHES, BUT NOT QUITE ALL OF THEM

When I started coaching, players could only pitch a certain number of innings per week, to protect players from pitching too much and damaging their arms. In other words, there had to be a system in place to prevent coaches who only cared about winning from riding their star pitcher until his arm was ready to fall off. This was a good idea, but since throwing two pitches or twenty-two all counted as pitching one inning, at some point, it was changed to a pitch count.

Great idea, except now coaches had to count pitches. Since coaches don't always trust each other, both teams would usually count their opponent's pitches as well as their own. Sometimes coaches didn't bother to count the pitches of the other team if they trusted the other coach to be honest, which was not always the case. I've heard coaches "confessing" more than once, "If I see the other team's not counting my team's pitches, I might 'forget' to click the pitch counter a few times, especially if my pitcher's cruising or it's a close game."

If a pitcher is limited to sixty pitches or eighty-five pitches, and the coach "forgets" to count a dozen or so pitches, it may help him win the game. But is a coach outsmarting the system that's been put in place to protect young arms really in the best interests of the players?

Absolutely not! This is another example of ruthless coaches doing whatever it takes to win, even if they're possibly harming a player in the process. Some coaches don't care if having their eleven-year-old ace pitcher throw too many pitches makes him need Tommy John surgery as a teenager, if it helps the coach win games now.

ANOTHER WAY COACHES BEND THE RULES: "QUICK PITCHING"

This is sometimes done by overly competitive coaches, often at younger age levels. To give their pitcher an advantage over the batter, they'll have him pitch before the batter is completely ready for the pitch. There's a lot of "gray area" in this rule. Baseball rules state that pitches can't be thrown until the batter is "reasonably set" in the batter's box, which is a very loosely defined term.

Some coaches have pitchers throw the pitch as soon as the batter's feet are in the batter's box, which is not being "reasonably set." Being "reasonably set" may take a few more seconds. If a pitcher throws while the batter isn't set, they have a big advantage over the batter. Some coaches train their pitchers to do this, which is against the rules and potentially dangerous if the batter isn't even looking up and the pitch comes right at his head. As an umpire, whenever I see attempts of a "quick pitch" happen, I tell the pitcher and his manager the pitch is not to be thrown until the batter has his feet set in the box *and* is looking up and making eye contact with the pitcher.

When pitchers work quickly, it moves the game along and keeps fielders more focused than when a pitcher works slowly. There is, however, a big difference between pitching quickly and the dangerous, illegal practice of quick pitching.

JUST POLITICS AS USUAL: COACHES SHOWING FAVORITISM

(Contributed by Miles in Connecticut)

Miles, a Connecticut parent, has a son named Jason. He was a good catcher as a nine- and ten-year-old and loved the involvement catchers have in the game. In 2015, after asking his new manager, when he moved up to the eleven and twelve age group, when he could catch, Jason got an answer of, "Sorry, Al's my catcher for the next two years."

Al was the son of his assistant coach. The manager and coach were both good friends and political allies, each holding multiple positions, including the two highest-ranking positions in the league.

After a practice, Miles approached Jason's manager, politely asking him, "Did you tell Jason he'll never be able to catch?"

"That's right," he said. "Al's my catcher for the next two years."

"That doesn't sound very fair," Miles countered, "considering this is a recreational league. Besides, he only has two years before moving on to Babe Ruth. If he doesn't catch for two years, he'll never be ready to catch there. How can you only have one catcher? The same kid can't catch every game."

"Yes, he can," the manager replied. "Al's my catcher for the next two years, and I don't appreciate you telling me how to run my team."

And the response from Miles to that was, "I'm not telling you how to run your team, I'm just asking you to be fair."

Miles asked around, thinking this was not fair, and was told there was a process to follow for resolving disagreements. He had to "follow the chain of command," starting at the bottom and working his way up. Seemed easy, as he certainly wasn't making an unreasonable request. The "chain of command" process to resolve disputes went as follows:

1. Try to resolve the problem with the team manager. Well, that failed!
2. Next in the chain of command was the director of the eleven- and twelve-year-old's league. Only problem, the league director is Al's dad, the manager's buddy. Since his kid is the "catcher for the next two years," even less progress was made with him!
3. Continuing up the chain of command meant bringing his grievance to the vice president of the league, who also happened to be Al's dad. So much for that!

Hearing this story from Miles about these coaches wearing several different hats reminded me of two goofy TV sitcoms I used to watch in the 1960s. *Petticoat Junction* and *Green Acres* were set in the mythical town of Hooterville. The town of Hooterville was completely run by Sam Drucker who, like these two coaches, wore many hats. Sam Drucker was mayor, owned the town's general store, was postmaster, and justice of the peace. Sam constantly took off one hat and put on another when switching from one job to another. That must have been what Miles felt like after dealing with these coaches who both wore multiple hats.

After getting nowhere, as a last resort, Miles finally went to the head guy. He was done fooling around. He took his complaint all the way to the top dog, the big Kahuna, the Grand Poobah, el Presidente, the number one person running the league.

El Presidente had an uncanny resemblance to the team manager. Who could have guessed? It was the same guy! To nobody's surprise, his reply to Miles was, "Sorry, Al's my catcher for the next two years."

As stated earlier, how could mixing politics with baseball possibly NOT screw things up?

COACHES WHO ARGUE WITH UMPIRES

(Contributed by Ethan from New Hampshire)

As a coach, I tried to respect the umpire, even when I thought the call was wrong. Now, as an umpire, I'm certain there's never been a game played in baseball history at any level where everyone agreed with every call made by umpires. Whether it's ten-year-olds or the pros, being able to think "the umpire blew the call" is part of what makes baseball so much fun to watch. It's part of the game, but your opinion must be kept to yourself.

Umpires expect disagreements with safe/out calls, or balls and strikes, and will put up with "grumbling" to a certain extent, but some coaches don't know when to stop. Some coaches seem like they were born to argue with umpires. They're like the "complainers" mentioned earlier who do nothing but complain. All some coaches do is disagree and argue with umpires the whole game.

As far as they're concerned, the umpire is the enemy, and from the moment the game starts, they "ride the umpire" and never stop. They think this will intimidate the umpire and close calls will go their way. Usually, the opposite happens. The umpires either get so sick of hearing the coach complain and call everything against him, or they eject the coach from the game.

In 2012, Ethan umpired a "tiebreaker" game in New Hampshire at the end of the regular season. Two teams had identical records, and it was decided these two teams would play a game to determine the number one seed for the playoffs.

Talk about making simple things complicated! How about just flipping a coin? When two teams finish with identical regular season records, if you don't want to just toss a coin, there are numerous "tiebreakers" that can be used to decide who finished first and who finished second. You can see who won the most games when the two teams played each other, or who scored the most runs when they played each other. But actually playing another game to decide this was ridiculous. Who came up with that brilliant idea?

In this game, one of the managers lived to argue with umpires. The sole purpose for his existence, the only reason Coach Phil was born, was to argue with umpires.

He argued that the other team wasn't ready to start on time, that there weren't enough baseballs, the baseballs were the wrong brand, the field was in lousy shape, and the rules about who could pitch in this game were wrong. Umpires didn't make rules about who was eligible to pitch and did not cut the grass improperly or provide the baseballs, but he acted as if the umpires did. The whole game, he commented on every pitch and call. "It was high; it was low. It was outside; it was inside. How could that be a strike? It was right down the middle; how could that be a ball? He beat the throw by a mile. How could he be out? How could you call him safe? He was clearly out; it wasn't even close!"

Ethan and Blake, the umpires, tried to ignore him, until near the end of the game when a strange play happened.

Phil's team was up by one run with two outs and the tying run on third in the bottom half of the final inning. Phil had his pitcher intentionally walk the other team's best hitter. This happened back when intentional walks still required a pitcher to throw four balls. With a count on the batter of three balls and no strikes, the intentional ball four sailed over the catcher's head to the backstop. The runner on third broke for the plate. The catcher ran, grabbed, and tossed the ball to the pitcher covering the plate. The runner slid in safely, just under the tag, with the tying run. The batter who took the wild pitch for ball four went to second base as his teammate scored.

Coach Phil charged onto the field, getting right into Ethan's face, screaming, "He was out, how could you not see that? You guys are the two worst f-----g umpires I've ever seen!"

Most umpires ignore a lot, but not someone swearing at them. "YOU'RE OUT OF HERE!" shouted Ethan. The runner on second scored on a walk-off single by the next batter to defeat Phil's team. After being ejected from the game, Phil was suspended for the playoffs and removed as a manager by the league. This was the tipping point for a league that was tired of his antics, and the constant complaints about him from parents and umpires. Ethan, Blake, and any umpire who had ever worked Coach Phil's games were ecstatic. Another ruthless coach bites the bust!

COACHES WHO DON'T KNOW WHAT THEY DON'T KNOW

As a veteran youth umpire, I see both experienced coaches and new ones. Although baseball is said to be "a simple kid's game," it has a lot of rules, some of which don't come into play very often. Coaches are expected to know the rules, especially if they're going to argue with an umpire about a ruling they disagree with.

Most umpires are happy to explain any rule that a coach isn't sure of. If a coach asks me to explain the intricate details of the "infield fly rule" or the "slide or avoid contact rule," I will gladly help clear up the mystery. Here are examples of basic rules some coaches don't know, yet still argue about:

– It's common knowledge that if the third out of an inning is a "force play," and a runner, probably on third base, crosses the plate before a force out is made, the run does not count.

In a game in 2022, a team had two outs and a runner on third base. The batter hit a grounder to the shortstop. An off-target throw caused the first baseman to come off first base to catch the throw, but he made a "swipe tag" to retire the batter before he reached first base. The runner on third crossed the plate just before the play was made on the batter at first base. As the base umpire, my call was "OUT AT

FIRST ON THE TAG!" That was the third out, ending the inning.

Immediately, the assistant coach in charge of the scorebook for the offensive team yells over to me, "The run counts, right, Blue?"

I was a bit surprised by the question, but just replied, "No, coach, the run doesn't count because the third out was a force play."

"But you said he was out on the tag, so it wasn't a force play, and the run should count," he said, his voice taking on a more argumentative tone.

"Coach, I'm sorry, even though the batter was tagged, it's still considered a force play, the run doesn't count, and we're done talking about this." His manager finally stepped in and told him I was right and to stop arguing about it.

– If a batter hits a clean gap shot to left center and runs into second base standing up just before the throw arrives, the defensive coach sometimes argues, "The runner should be out because he didn't slide into the base."

– If a batter hits a grounder that bounced off the plate when he first hit the pitch, and he makes it to first base, the defensive coach argues, "Hey, that should be a foul ball because it bounced off the plate."

– If a runner is stealing and the batter swings and "foul tips" the ball into the catcher's glove, and the catcher holds the ball, it's like a swing and miss, the ball is live, and runners may advance. Several times I've heard a defensive coach incorrectly say, "Hey, Blue, the runner who stole second has to go back because of the foul tip."

– If there are less than two outs and runners on first and second, or all three bases, the "infield fly rule" could apply if the batter hits a fly ball that should be a routine catch requiring "ordinary effort," meaning the fielder gets under the fly ball and is ready to catch it. It must be a fly ball, not a "flare," line drive, or popped-up bunt. Several times a year, coaches ask why I didn't call "INFIELD FLY, THE BATTER IS OUT" on flares no more than ten feet in the air that fall between two infielders, popped-up attempted bunts, or when an infielder can't reach a pop-up in the back of the infield when bases are loaded, and the infielders are "playing in."

– If a pitch bounces and hits the batter in the leg, the batter is awarded first base. The pitch hitting the ground before hitting the batter is irrelevant. I've had defensive coaches say, "Hey, ump, the batter shouldn't get first base because the pitch hit the ground first before hitting him." In a game in 2022, I almost ejected a manager who argued with me when this happened. At first, he questioned me, then became more argumentative as our conversation went on.

Coach: "Blue, why does the batter get first? Didn't you see that the pitch hit the ground first before it hit the batter?"

Me: "Coach, it doesn't matter that the pitch hit the ground first, it still hit the batter."

Coach: "Are you kidding? Of course, it matters."

Me: "No, it doesn't matter. The ball isn't dead just because a pitch hits the ground. If a pitch bounces before reaching the plate, and the batter swings and hits it over the fence, it's still a home run, right?"

The coach rolled his eyes and became angry. "Yes, but that's different, and you know I'm right!"

"Okay, this discussion is over," I said. "I've explained the rule to you, and you don't believe me, so look up the rule and you'll see that I'm right."

He threw up his hands in frustration, rolled his eyes

again, shook his head, turned, and walked away, probably thinking I was just another umpire who didn't know what he was doing. If he kept insisting I was wrong, I probably would've ejected him for an argument that was completely unnecessary.

One of his assistant coaches checked on the rule and told the manager that I was right. The manager, being a bit of a jerk, never apologized to me, and because of a rule he didn't know, the game was delayed, there was a needless argument with an umpire, and since he was defiant about it, was almost ejected. So, coaches, before arguing with umpires about rules, make sure you know what you're talking about. If you disagree with what the umpire says, please be open to the possibility that the umpire might be right, and you might be wrong.

Most umpires don't mind explaining rules, but they do mind when coaches argue about rules they don't have a clue about.

COACHES WHO TRY TO "APPEAL" EVERYTHING

One of the most misunderstood rules by youth baseball coaches is the "appeal rule," and the process of how to make an appeal. There are situations in baseball that require a coach to ask the umpire to make a ruling on something the coach saw. This is called "making an appeal." There is a proper way a coach must make an appeal, and there are only certain situations where a coach is even allowed to make an appeal.

If an umpire notices certain violations, such as a runner missing a base, he doesn't say or do anything unless a coach or player brings it to his attention and makes "an appeal" in the proper manner. Coaches must follow an exact procedure to make an "appeal," and if they don't do it properly, the umpire will deny the appeal, which often leads to an unhappy coach and an ensuing argument. An appeal can only be made while the ball is live and in play, not after "time" is called, and must be made before a pitch is thrown to the next batter.

If there are two or more umpires in a game, sometimes "an appeal" is asking a second umpire to validate or overturn a call made by the first umpire. Only certain plays can be appealed.

Plays that can be appealed:

- "Check swings" if the plate umpire called a ball.
- Runner, who is "tagging up" after a catch is made, leaves a base too soon.
- Batting out of order.
- Runner missing a base.

Plays that cannot be appealed:

- Pitches where the batter tried to check his swing, but the plate umpire said he swung.
- Balls and strikes called by the plate umpire.
- Any umpire judgment call, such as a safe or out call at any base.

What is most often appealed by coaches in youth baseball? By far, the most common appeal is for umpire judgment calls. In almost every youth game, there's a close play on the bases. The base umpire makes his safe or out call, and a coach disagrees. Despite being sixty to one hundred or more feet away, the coach feels he saw the play differently than the umpire who was six feet away. He pipes up, "I want to appeal that call," or if he wants to be polite will ask, "Can you please ask your partner for help on that call? He might have had a better view of it than you did."

What he really is saying to the umpire is more like, "Are you f-----g blind? You called him out and he was safe by a mile! I want your partner to overrule you even though he was nowhere near the play, and you were right on top of it!"

What the coach is trying to do is get a "second opinion"

from the umpire who didn't make the call, and if the second umpire agrees with the coach, have him convince the first umpire to change his call. Coaches can't make an "appeal" to get a second opinion from another umpire simply because they disagree with a judgement call made by the first umpire. It's not like being able to seek a second opinion about how to fix your knee pain when the first doctor says he wants to operate, and you don't like that suggestion.

When an umpire tells a coach, "You can't appeal umpire judgment calls," it really makes them mad because coaches think they're always right and umpires are always wrong. To pacify an irate coach, umpires often have a prearranged agreement with each other. When a coach makes an appeal for something that can't be appealed, rather than further irritating the coach by telling him he can't appeal the call, the "dog and pony show" begins!

The umpires get together where nobody can hear what they say. They pretend to discuss the play, and after a few seconds of talking about the hot-looking babe in the third row of the bleachers, or anything *other* than the play, they confirm that the original call stands. For some reason, going through this charade where the umpires meet, pretend to discuss the call, and wind up with the same result usually satisfies most coaches.

So please, coaches, know the rules on how to make a proper appeal, and what situations can and cannot be appealed. The games run more smoothly with less unnecessary friction between coaches and umpires.

COACHES WHO DON'T KNOW WHEN TO QUIT (LORD, HAVE MERCY)

Baseball has a reputation for being a slow game, and sometimes it is. Although leagues try to put together teams that will all be competitive, at times one team is far superior to another. To make these games less painful, most leagues use what is called a "mercy rule." For example, if a game is supposed to go seven innings, the mercy rule might state that if one team is ahead by fifteen runs after four innings, or ten runs after five innings, the game is over. Without this, some lopsided games would literally never end.

In 2016, I umpired a game of high school-aged players, where one team was really good, and the other was horrible. The score was 11-0 after one inning. Normally these games take about two hours to play seven innings. The first three innings took two hours, and the score was 25-1.

Before the fourth inning, I approached the manager who was winning, and asked, "The mercy rule kicks in after four innings, right?"

"Ugh, sorry," he replied, "there's no mercy rule in this league. If you can talk the other manager into calling it quits, that'd be fine with us. We've played three innings in the time it usually takes to play seven! You can try, but we know him and doubt he'll agree to end the game early."

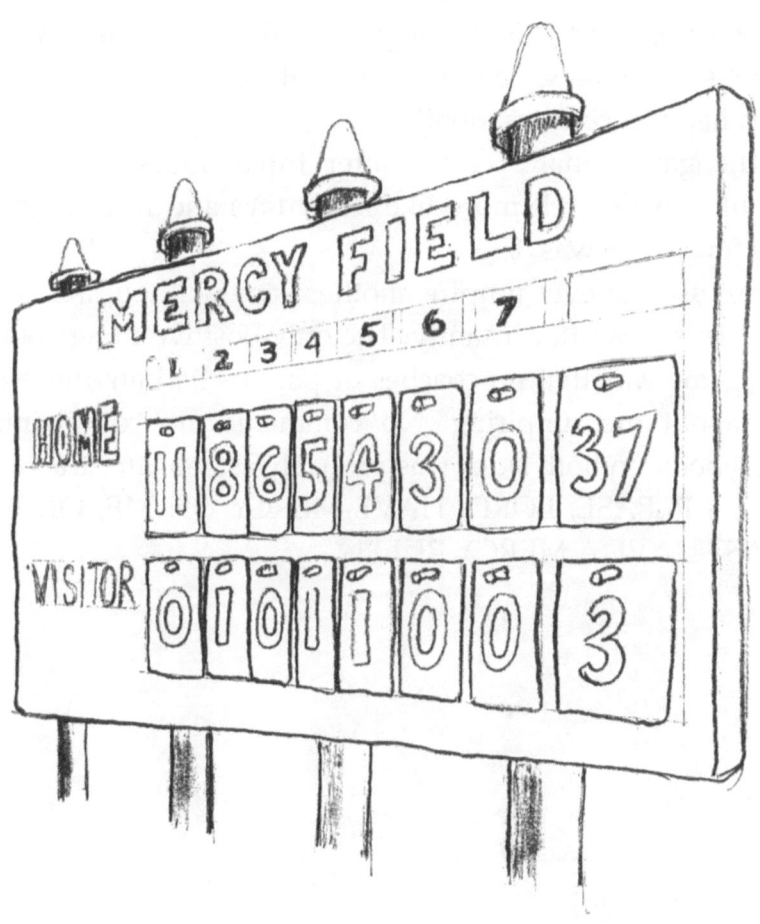

I approached the losing manager and diplomatically said, "Coach, I know there's no mercy rule, but you're behind by twenty-four runs. How about if we play one more inning, and if the score doesn't change, can we call it a day?"

He looked at me like I had two heads, possibly three. "This is baseball," he said, "and the way I was taught, whether you win or lose, you play hard until the end. We're going seven innings, and I don't want my guys to know we even had this conversation!"

The game finally ended after three hours and forty minutes, which felt more like forty days and forty nights. The final score was 37-3.

I refused to ever umpire another game without a mercy rule. This was utter insanity. The only positive thing about this game was that no coaches or parents had anything to say about the umpiring. No comments, no complaints. Everybody on both sides was probably asleep after the first inning! PLEASE, LORD, HAVE MERCY ON ME, OR AT LEAST HAVE A MERCY RULE!

BUT SIR...

Sometimes umpires deal with coaches that complain about everything. Coach Phil, who I referred to earlier, was anything but respectful. Other coaches still complain but are so overly respectful in the way they tell you they aren't impressed with your umpiring skills, that it's quite comical.

As a new umpire, like any new job, you start at the bottom. The first game I ever umpired in 2008 was a summer league game of nine-year-olds in the "9B" division. The "B" doesn't stand for "bad," but in this game, it could have. This division was for players who didn't make the "A" travel team.

Maybe my umpiring was horrible. It probably wasn't great since it was my first game! A coach of one team didn't like my strike zone or any call I made and constantly complained but did it so politely it was hard not to laugh.

He prefaced every complaint with a smile and the words, "But, sir":

"But, sir, you called strike three on a pitch at his eyes."

"But, sir, you called strike three on a pitch at his ankles."

"But, sir, you called ball four and the pitch was perfect."

"But, sir, you called him out and he clearly beat the throw."

"But, sir, you called him safe when he was clearly out."

"But, sir..."

"But, sir..."

I feared for my sanity as he tried to smile and "but, sir" me into submission. It was a bit annoying, but good for a few laughs after he smiled and said "but, sir" to me for about the thirty-seventh time.

I'M REPORTING YOU TO THE LEAGUE FOR DISRESPECTING ME!

(Contributed by Kirk from New York)

After Kirk stopped playing baseball at fourteen, he became a youth umpire and worked games in the town league in New York where he used to play. This is how many umpires get their start, working local games involving younger players. One coach in the league, Coach Steve, was known for "bullying" young umpires, trying to get close calls to go his way.

Kirk, like most of his fellow youth umpires, never liked working this coach's games. Kirk was in his second year of umpiring and had umpired several of Steve's games. He'd complain constantly about calls, try to intimidate umpires, and often reminded the umpires how many calls they got wrong during games. In one game, it was not going well for Steve's team, and he was all over the umpires. After a close play at the plate went against his team, he stormed out to the plate, took off his cap, and slammed it on the ground while yelling at Kirk that it was impossible to blow a call that badly. He was furious!

Kirk, an unusually confident fifteen-year-old, looked at this big, intimidating thirty-eight-year-old who was waving his arms and jumping up and down like a complete idiot. Kirk started laughing. That got Coach Steve even madder.

"ARE YOU LAUGHING AT ME?" he screamed at the young umpire. "I'm reporting you to the head of the league for being completely unprofessional and disrespecting me."

Not to be outdone, Kirk said back, "You're right, coach, I'm sorry, I shouldn't be laughing, but you have no idea how foolish you look screaming at a fifteen-year-old umpire over a play in a nine-year-old's game." Kirk pulled out his phone and said, "Why don't I call the head of the league for you? You can report me for laughing at you after you screamed at me, or should I say you 'disrespected ME' constantly for five innings. Let's see what he says. Should we do that, or would you prefer to stay in the dugout without saying another word for the rest of the game?"

No answer from Coach Steve. He'd acted like an idiot, but he wasn't stupid. He knew he was about to be ejected from the game by a fifteen-year-old umpire. He turned around, went to his dugout, and was not heard from for the rest of the game. After the game, Kirk reported to his umpire supervisor how badly the coach had behaved, which he was supposed to do if coaches gave the umpires any trouble.

The next day, Kirk found out Coach Steve was suspended by the league for a week. Well done, Kirk! You made umpires everywhere proud. We need more good, young umpires like you, cleaning up youth baseball, one bad coach at a time!

WHERE HAVE ALL THE UMPIRES GONE?

Not too many years ago, there were plenty of umpires and officials for all youth sports. Many officials didn't get to work as many games as they wanted to. That situation has completely changed. A serious problem currently exists in baseball and all youth sports, and that is a shortage of officials.

Coaches like Steve and Phil, as well as outspoken parents, are driving umpires away. A 2019 report carried by newspapers nationwide spotlighted a critical shortage of both amateur baseball umpires and officials in all youth sports. The problem exists at all levels and ages of youth and high school sports—and baseball in particular.

Most amateur officials do this as a "second job." Like me, they officiate baseball or any sport because they love the game. They earn extra money doing something that's fun and different from their regular job.

The reason for the shortage of officials is clear: As youth sports officials get older, they work fewer games and eventually retire. Not enough new, younger officials are coming in to replace older ones that are leaving.

It seems like several times a year, we hear about a youth sports official being physically assaulted. In 2022, there were two incidents I heard about, and there probably were others.

In April of 2022, a Texas youth umpire was shoved to the ground by a coach who'd been ejected after arguing about a "safe" call on a play at the plate in a game of nine- and ten-year-old players. The umpire's head struck the ground when he fell backward. After reportedly being down for about ten minutes, the umpire was taken to the hospital on a stretcher with a possible concussion.

Several weeks later, in June, a seventy-two-year-old New Jersey youth umpire was punched in the face by a forty-year-old coach he'd ejected from a 13U game for using foul language. Whatever the umpire earned for working this game—sixty, eighty, a hundred dollars, or whatever it was—no amount of money was worth this. The umpire sustained a concussion and broken jaw, which required extensive surgery to repair. Reportedly, some parents were overheard in the stands saying things about the umpire like, "He deserved it."

While incidents like this don't happen every day, when they do, it doesn't encourage anyone to rush to become a youth sports official. While physical assaults of youth officials don't occur regularly, disagreements that escalate into verbal assaults happen far too often. Potential new officials are being driven away, and veteran officials are giving it up, tired of the aggravation and abuse they take from coaches and parents.

As this book was about to go to press, on January 31, 2023, a brawl broke out involving spectators at a middle school basketball game in northern Vermont. Parents of players spilled onto the court and a sixty-year-old man who was involved in the fight died later that night. While details about the cause of his death or what started the fight had not been released, this is one more incident of behavior by obnoxious parents contributing to the shortage of officials in youth sports. While no officials appeared to be targeted in this incident, why would anyone considering becoming an official want to put themselves in potential situations where they might get caught in the crossfire of something like this?

Not enough young people want to become officials, even though the money's decent, and you're involved in sports you enjoy. In some sports, like baseball and football, you get to work outside, and for teenagers, it beats working for minimum wage in a fast-food joint.

In 2011, the umpire association I belong to had 175 members. Eleven years later, our membership was down to ninety-six, with an average age over sixty. We have some younger umpires but need many more. I've seen promising young umpires take training classes, work for a few years, then get sick of hearing coaches and parents screaming at them whenever calls don't go their way. My son was an excellent young umpire, starting when he was thirteen, and giving it up when he was twenty-two. In his words, "The money wasn't bad, but it just wasn't worth listening to people complain all the time."

Not all young umpires are like Kirk. Kirk was an extremely confident young umpire who wasn't intimidated by a coach trying to take advantage of his age and inexperience. He thought it was funny when a coach would "flip out" over something that happened in a nine-year-old's baseball game. It didn't bother him, which is great, but it's rare to have that attitude. Most young umpires, even those who can handle overly competitive coaches, don't want the aggravation. In too many cases, the way Coach Steve treated Kirk makes most newer umpires find another way to make money.

Because of the umpire shortage, many freshman and junior varsity high school games have only one umpire. Using only one umpire on the big diamond is unfair to the players, as there's always a close pickoff play or steal on the bases that the umpire behind the plate can't see that well. In 2022, some sub-varsity games were officiated by assistant coaches standing behind the pitcher because no umpires were available.

Some high school varsity games in recent years had to be rescheduled due to a lack of umpires. In 2021 and 2022, umpire assignors who provide umpires to local youth rec leagues and competitive club leagues were often begging umpires to work more games than they wanted to so games wouldn't be canceled due to a lack of officials. This happened in my area, and all over the country. Many times, on weekends, I'd be scheduled to work two games Saturday and two games Sunday and would be asked to work extra games because there weren't enough umpires for all the scheduled games.

That's why my wife calls herself a "baseball widow" at times during the baseball season!

For many years, I ran a youth umpire program, training teenagers to officiate games for eight-to-twelve-year-olds in recreational leagues. We'd employ thirteen-to-eighteen-year-old former players. At one time, I had fifty kids umpiring, and couldn't find enough games for everyone. Five years later, the number fell to fifteen, because the young umpires couldn't deal with coaches and parents acting like every game was game seven of the world championship series. They'd rather make less money at a restaurant or bagging groceries. Nothing wrong with those jobs, but for a kid who loves baseball to rather work there, something's not right.

Youth umpire programs like the one I ran are the "pipeline" where umpires of the future come from. All over the country, this "pipeline" is drying up. Teenagers that love baseball try their hand at umpiring. In the past, many found they liked it and continued umpiring beyond their local town leagues. I sometimes umpire recreational league games and mentor a youth umpire working the game with me. Most thirteen-to-fourteen-year-old umpires are inexperienced, and many get rattled when a coach who disagrees with a call lets them know about it. In recent years, too many new young umpires have gotten fed up with coaches bullying them and parents abusing them.

The umpire shortage is now a crisis, and the average age of officials keeps climbing. The problem exists across all youth sports. Recently someone was telling me about the referees who officiate his twelve-year-old son's basketball league.

"These guys are so old, they can barely make it up and down the floor! Why aren't there any younger refs?" he asked me.

Coaches and parents often view officials as "the enemy," but games don't happen without them. I haven't mentioned umpires being driven away because of problems with players. While there are occasional player issues, the overwhelming majority of problems officials have in all youth sports are with coaches and parents, not players.

So, here's a stern warning to outspoken coaches and parents: There are more youth baseball games every year, and fewer umpires to work them. The umpire shortage was getting bad in 2019, and COVID-19 made it worse.

Part of what makes baseball so much fun is being able to think "the umpire blew the call!" Even though in this country we have the constitutional right of "Freedom of Speech," this right does not apply in youth baseball games! You can think whatever you want but you must keep your thoughts to yourself, even when you completely disagree with the umpire. So please, coaches and parents, on behalf of umpires and all youth sports officials, WAKE UP AND SHUT UP!

UMPIRING IN THE AGE OF COVID-19

In 2020, COVID-19 changed the world, including the sports world. The 2020 baseball season was delayed, as were other pro sports, and shortened seasons were played in empty stadiums without fans. The Summer Olympics in Japan were postponed for a year. Spring school sports were canceled. Youth baseball, normally April–July, ran July–October. Since baseball has very little physical contact between players, it was one of the first youth sports to be able to resume, although with some modifications.

Since many people worked from home, and students attended school remotely from March to June, everyone was thrilled to be out of their homes doing something "normal" again. Players and coaches had to stay six feet apart and wear masks. No hugging or high-fiving was allowed, and after games, opposing players would "wave" or "tip their caps" to the other team rather than shake hands.

Teams provided their own baseballs, so pitchers were only handling baseballs that their team was touching. Umpires didn't handle baseballs. While in theory, this sounded good, it became a moot point quickly when the first batter up would hit a foul ball. A spectator would chase it down, and toss it to another spectator, who would then toss it to the coach of the wrong team, who would toss it to the correct coach. In less than a minute, the baseball had been touched by way too many hands. So that strategy didn't quite work.

Balls and strikes were called from behind the pitcher, which is tough to do, especially on a big diamond where you'd be seventy feet away. With the plate ump in the middle of the field, he'd handle calls on bases. If there was a second umpire, he'd usually be off to the side in the home plate area to handle fair and foul ball calls and plays at the plate. While this worked to a certain degree, it wasn't ideal.

At first, everyone was so glad to be playing baseball that nobody complained about anything. That lasted a week or two, and then the honeymoon ended. Umpires got as much grief from coaches and parents as ever, sometimes more because nobody could accurately call balls and strikes from behind the mound.

In 2021, we resumed playing and officiating baseball the "normal" way. Unfortunately, COVID reduced umpire ranks even further. Many umpires who "opted out" in 2020 never returned. With fewer new umpires coming on board recently because of the abuse officials endure from coaches and parents, the umpire shortage is now worse than ever.

So, on behalf of my fellow umpires, I am again pleading with coaches and parents who make life miserable for umpires: STOP making umpires give up the game! KEEP your opinions to yourself! Whether you like it or not, you can't play games without umpires. YOU NEED US!

FIGHTING IN YOUTH SPORTS

I'm talking, once again, about coaches and parents. In youth sports, players are rarely the problem. Sometimes it gets ugly, and even deadly.

In a Boston suburb in 2000, a youth hockey referee was killed right after a game ended. The parent of a player disagreed with how the game was officiated. When the 150-pound referee came off the ice, he was ambushed, thrown down, and pinned to the floor by a 270-pound parent. With the much larger attacker kneeling on his chest, the referee couldn't move and was literally beaten to death after officiating a ten-year-old's game.

This incident made national news. After appeals, in January 2002, the assailant was convicted of manslaughter and served eight years in prison. Until this happened in another Boston suburb only forty miles from where I lived, my feeling was, *That sort of thing would never happen here; stuff like that only happens in other places.*

While I've never witnessed anything like that, I've seen minor scuffles and have had to stop arguments that were about to escalate into fights. Again, no players, just parents or coaches.

EVERYONE NEEDS TO RELAX. IT'S JUST A BUNCH OF KIDS PLAYING A GAME!

There is no excuse for any of this. Parents and coaches wouldn't let their kids get in fights, but they will fight. What's wrong with these people?

In April of 2002, I was about to coach my first real game after a year of T-ball and a year of coach pitching. It was three months after the manslaughter verdict was issued for the hockey incident. My eight-year-old daughter (now thirty-one) was playing softball, and I was a coach for her team of eight- and nine-year-olds. The first game of the season was about to start, with both teams on their benches. I looked across the field and saw something strange.

The manager and assistant coach of the other team were pushing and shoving each other, I assumed "playfully"? At first, I figured they were fooling around, just "boys being boys."

Quickly the pushing and shoving became anything but playful. A big roundhouse right fist headed for the jaw of one coach, who ducked to avoid the punch, and charged into the chest of the other coach, knocking him to the ground, where they rolled around, wrestling for a few seconds. They were quickly separated by horrified parents, one being the league commissioner, as the stunned eight- and nine-year-old girls looked on.

The commissioner escorted both coaches away, and two other parents had to step in to coach the team. Both coaches got two-week suspensions. Something about this fight was unusual, because when there's a fight in sports, you'd expect it to be between people from opposing sides. These two guys were both on the same team! The cause of the fight was never revealed, but I didn't care what the reason was. I thought this sort of thing was only supposed to happen "in other places," not here. I was shocked, and don't remember a thing about this game other than the pre-game fireworks!

A MOST AWKWARD TRIP TO THE DRUGSTORE

The story continues! The fight before the softball game was the talk of the town all week. Everybody heard about it, and this was in pre–cell phone and social media days. I can't even imagine the tweets and videos if this had happened twenty years later.

Two days after the game, I went to my local drugstore to fill a prescription. I walked up to the pharmacy counter, and my jaw dropped when I saw who'd be filling my prescription. The pharmacist was the wife of one of the coaches in the fight. I remembered seeing her at the game, as her daughter played on the other team. I think she was as shocked to see me as I was to see her. AWKWARD SILENCE! Neither of us knew what to say, so we both said nothing.

It probably took less than five minutes to fill the prescription, but it seemed to take days. I wanted to say something like, "Hey, Charlotte, I think your husband is a real jerk for getting in a fight at the ball field, don't you agree?"

I decided, for my own health and well-being, to keep quiet. It might not be wise to insult her husband since she could probably fill my prescription bottle with anything she wanted, and I'd never know the difference until I was dead! Probably a smart move on my part!

COACH JOE TRIES TO JOIN THE FIGHT CLUB

(Contributed by Willis in Alabama)

Willis was watching his nine-year-old son's game in Alabama in 2009. Coach Joe, the manager of the team playing against his son's team, didn't always get along with other coaches, and in this game, he went too far.

His team was losing badly, and Joe tried to start a fight with Frank, the coach of Willis's son. Frank wasn't doing anything wrong. His team was just playing better that day, but apparently, Joe thought Frank was trying to "run up the score."

In the middle of an inning, Joe sauntered over to Frank and said, "I'm sick and tired of your crap. C'mon, let's go — you and me, right here, right now!"

Bewildered, Frank shook his head in disbelief and said, "You want to have a fight with me over a nine-year-old's baseball game? You're crazy!" He turned and walked away.

Assistant coaches were ready to jump in between the two, but nothing happened, and the game continued. The next batter up for Frank's team was his own son. Joe called time and went to the mound. Joe's son was pitching. Frank wondered what Joe was up to. Although Joe gave instructions about how to pitch to the batter quietly, his son

reacted with a loud, emphatic "NO, I'M NOT DOING THAT!" which everybody heard.

Apparently, since Frank wouldn't fight Joe, the next best thing for Joe was to have his son intentionally hit Frank's son with a pitch! Although Frank didn't personally hear Joe say this, his runner on second base told him, after the inning, he overheard Coach Joe tell his son to "hit the batter." The way Joe's son reacted, it seemed like that was exactly what he was instructed to do.

Are you kidding? These are nine-year-olds, and he wants his pitcher—who's also his son—to intentionally hit the son of the opposing team's coach who refused to fight with him. What's wrong with this guy?

After the more sensible nine-year-old member of Joe's family refused to carry out Dad's idiotic orders, the game finished without further incidents. Thank goodness somebody in the family had a brain!

Horrified parents watching had witnessed this whole thing. Several reported the incident to the league's president that night, which Frank did as well. Frank spoke to Willis the day after the game telling him, "I'm forty years old and felt like I was back in grade school being challenged by the schoolyard bully. I couldn't believe he did this in front of a bunch of nine-year-olds!"

Coach Joe, a less than fabulous role model for children, was already "skating on thin ice" after another incident earlier in the season. This time he fell through the ice. After this offense, Joe was removed as manager and permanently banned from coaching in the league. Everywhere, good coaches like Frank, as well as umpires, were rejoicing as the career of yet another ruthless coach bites the dust!

THE CODE OF CONDUCT

What is this? In simple terms, it tells players, coaches, and spectators something they should already know: HOW TO BEHAVE! It states that players, coaches, spectators, and officials are to always treat each other with respect and practice good sportsmanship.

The code of conduct is, in my mind, a great thing. While it's all just common sense and courtesy, youth sports are taken so seriously by some adults that there needs to be written rules telling everyone how to behave. Most sports organizations have one, although parents and coaches who take things way too seriously say they were never told about it, or just don't care because it's never enforced.

For years, especially once I became an umpire, I pleaded with organizers of leagues where I worked for better enforcement of their code of conduct. I think every parent and coach should sign a form before every season, promising to abide by the terms.

Every year, I'd see or hear about at least one ugly incident, with a parent or coach screaming at a fifteen-year-old umpire, or one coach challenging another to a fight. In my two decades of coaching and umpiring, I've seen situations where parents were no longer allowed to sit in the stands and watch their sons' games because they just couldn't behave. Imagine behaving so badly, and doing it more than just once, that you get banned for life from watching your kid play baseball?

In recent years, I've noticed more communities putting up signs at baseball fields. Both in the dugouts, and near spectator-seating areas, signs are posted telling players, coaches, and spectators to behave. The signs would say something like, PLEASE BEHAVE PROPERLY AND SHOW RESPECT TO OUR PLAYERS, COACHES, AND UMPIRES AT ALL TIMES. ANYONE NOT BEHAVING PROPERLY WILL BE ASKED TO LEAVE THE PREMISES.

It shouldn't be necessary to post signs to tell supposedly intelligent adults to behave at their kid's baseball games, but unfortunately, it is!

MY YEARS AS A COACH AND MANAGER

"TORTURE BALL"/ "THERE'S NO CRYING IN BASEBALL!"

I coached and managed for ten years, starting with my daughter in T-ball. After a few days, I wanted to change the name of the game from T-ball to "TORTURE BALL." While five-year-olds are cute, for somebody who loves real baseball, coaching T-ball can be torture. When I was a kid, there was no T-ball, so I didn't play organized baseball until I was nine, and I was ready for it. Parents today sign up their future stars for Torture Ball before they are necessarily ready—and whether or not they show any interest.

T-ball is simple. You place the ball on a tee, give the kid a bat, and they swing at the ball. Seems easy enough. Some, at this age, are much better than others. Some swing five or six times before making contact with the ball. Some just knock over the tee and never actually hit the ball.

When they hit the ball, they run to first base while six fielders fight over the ball. When the next kid hits the ball, they run to the next base. This continues and when the last kid in the order comes up and hits the ball, everyone runs all the way around the bases. What fun!

At five and six, attention spans are short, and for fielders, there's not much to keep them occupied. There were boys and girls on my team. Girls would sometimes show off their newly painted fingernails to teammates.

In one game, I remember this poor little girl who picked up a grounder hit to her and started screaming, like she'd been hit in the face. I ran over thinking she was really hurt.

"What happened, Jenny, are you okay?" I asked.

Crying her eyes out, she said, "Coach, I just had my nails painted and I broke my nail!"

Hearing this, her mom came over, completely mortified, picked her daughter up, and said to me, "I think we're calling it a day." Probably wasn't a bad idea.

One of my favorite movie lines of all time was delivered by the drunk manager Jimmy Dugan, played by Tom Hanks, in the 1992 movie *A League of Their Own*. After yelling at one of his players and making her cry, he blurts out, "ARE YOU CRYING? YOU CAN'T CRY. THERE'S NO CRYING IN BASEBALL!" I guess little Jenny hadn't seen that movie yet.

TEAMWORK IN TORTURE BALL

One way infielders keep themselves busy when not much is happening during T-ball games is by digging in the dirt. Some players just push dirt around, but others build actual sand structures. I once witnessed, during a game, the second baseman and shortstop working together to build a city on the infield dirt. At any age, teamwork on a baseball field is a beautiful thing!

Parents would take nonstop pictures and videos to make sure none of the action would go without documentation for future generations to yawn over.

TWICE THE FUN OF ONE YEAR OF TORTURE BALL

The kids at this age are absolutely adorable, but one year of Torture Ball is enough for anyone. However, since my kids are five years apart, I got to coach Torture Ball again five years later. Lucky me!

On my second tour of Torture Ball duty, one player was light-years ahead of everyone else. Jack, who would become an outstanding ball player in a few years, played T-ball as a five-year-old.

Jack had three older brothers he played baseball with since learning to walk. At five, he had more skills than some players twice his age. He could already hit, catch, run, and throw. He even knew how to slide. Even though he was really into the game, it never bothered him that other kids could barely get the bat to make contact with a ball sitting on a tee. He didn't mind that others were more interested in building sandcastles in the infield or picking dandelions in the outfield. He never made fun of kids taking seven swings before dribbling the ball about six feet.

He patiently waited for his turn and would launch the ball over infielder's heads while everybody else barely reached the pitcher's mound. Coaches hoped he'd launch the ball over everyone so he wouldn't take the heads off any fielders while they worked tirelessly on their infield dirt construction projects.

Nobody had to tell Jack to run. He'd fly out of the batter's box, sprint full speed to first base, and overrun the base like he was trying to beat out a close play at first. He must have pretended that a fielder on the other team was paying attention and actually trying to throw him out. Some imagination!

Since nobody could take more than one base at a time, when the next batter hit, he'd be off on contact, running full speed, and sliding into second, third, or home. If he really wanted to have fun, he'd slide headfirst. We had to keep telling him not to do it because head-first sliding wasn't allowed until you were thirteen. He'd have the coaches and parents in stitches laughing at these outstanding slides in T-ball! Of course, there was no reason to slide, as fielders were too busy building sand structures. He just liked sliding and was very good at it! Jack kept my hopes alive for the future when I'd coach older kids who would have actual baseball skills.

"A" BALL, A.K.A. "COACH PITCH"

When players turned six, coaches pitched to the kids. The object for the coach pitching was to do anything in your power to hit the bat. With some kids, you'd stand close to where a pitcher would normally be. With others, you'd move in so close, you could almost touch the bat before you released the ball. Some kids showed promise; others were hopeless, clueless, or both. Although I'm not religious, I'd pray before every pitch to the baseball gods to PLEASE make this kid hit the ball, or at least make the ball hit the bat.

Some coaches were bolder than I was. One would kneel six feet from the batter and toss the ball at the swinging bat. If the kid hit the ball, the coach's face was history. If the bat slipped out of the batter's hands while swinging, the coach's face was also history.

Like T-ball, we didn't keep score, just tried to teach basic skills. At times, it seemed like the only areas where we could see major skill improvements were digging in the dirt and weed pulling. Improving actual baseball skills was going to take a while.

PARTICIPATION TROPHIES

It's always bugged me that trophies are given to all five-to-eight-year-old players just for showing up. Nobody needs a hunk of tin and plastic that sits on a shelf collecting dust. After a few years of collecting dust on a shelf, trophies get moved from a shelf to a drawer, and eventually wind up in a landfill. One league's equipment room had dozens of trophies because people never picked them up after the season. Stop wasting money on these dust collectors that nobody wants!

THE SOFTBALL YEARS

My softball coaching career was a brief two years as an assistant coach. My daughter played softball at eight and nine after playing a year of Torture Ball and a year of Coach Pitch. The manager I worked under was a great guy and excellent coach, who I enjoyed working with and taught me a lot about the game. After two seasons, my daughter decided softball just wasn't her thing. Barely five feet tall as an adult, she was so *tiny* at that age, that she'd be walked almost every time she batted, as her strike zone was about half the size of a postage stamp.

One of the best players in the league was a terrific hitter who also had a cannon of an arm, even at nine years old. She could easily make great throws from third to first, or from the outfield to home plate. Lizzie had the strongest throwing arm I'd ever seen on someone that age. She loved the game, but her coach really wanted her to pitch, which she had trouble doing, and didn't seem to like very much.

If she could have pitched overhand, like you do in baseball, Lizzie would probably have done well, but softball is pitched underhand. Pitching fast in softball requires a difficult windmill windup motion, which involves a lot of balance and complicated mechanics. This is difficult, especially for young players. She couldn't seem to master this complex technique needed to pitch effectively. Even with her coach encouraging her and reminding her of things like "stay balanced, stay square, drive from the legs," it just wasn't working. She was an outstanding softball player, but pitching in softball is just not something everyone can do. Even for an excellent player like Lizzie, she didn't pitch very well consistently.

Lizzie didn't hit the strike zone as often as her coach would have liked. Her pitchers were often high or low, and sometimes rolled on the ground like she was bowling. She walked a lot of batters and, unfortunately, also hit a lot of batters.

In one game, she hit a batter in the ankle, and this girl was a figure skater practicing countless hours every day. Her parents were real "pushers and grinders," proclaiming that their daughter was a future Olympic-figure skater. After getting hit in the ankle by a pitch from Lizzie, Shelly was down on the ground, unable to walk. Her father raced onto the field, picked her up, and carried off his fallen future Olympian, while he screamed at Lizzie's coach, "That girl shouldn't be pitching, she hits everybody and if Shelly can't skate because of this, you're going to be in trouble because this is your fault!"

With all that drama, and feeling terrible about hurting Shelly, Lizzie was crying her eyes out and her coach took her out of the game. Shelly was taken for X rays, which were negative, but her parents wouldn't let her play softball again. Shelly gave up figure skating a couple of years later when she was eleven because "it wasn't fun anymore." What a surprise! Lizzie continued playing softball into high school and was much happier when her coach stopped asking her to pitch.

I also witnessed, during my brief softball coaching career, a fight between two coaches, which was described earlier. While coaches or anyone fighting in sports is never a good thing, usually it's because two teams don't like each other or some other foolish reason. I never found out what prompted these two coaches, who were both on the same team, to start pushing, shoving, and swinging at each other before this game even got started.

That was one of the first of about three hundred times in my coaching and umpiring career when I said to myself, "Now I've seen everything."

I was wrong. I was just getting started on "seeing everything."

COACHING SEVEN- AND EIGHT-YEAR-OLDS

At this level, coaching became slightly more interesting. There were signs of hope, where players had some throwing, catching, and hitting skills.

The game and rules were modified for the skill level of players this age. Coaches were allowed to be on the field during the games to instruct players as things happened during games.

Because so few kids this age can pitch, pitchers were used only for two innings. If we survived two innings of kids pitching, which usually took forever, we'd use a pitching machine for the rest of the game. The pitching machine was great. Every pitch was the same. Hitters were swinging and hitting, and fielders tried to make plays. Games moved along using the pitching machine, unlike when pitchers walked batter after batter.

Most pitchers couldn't reach the plate, so they'd be allowed to move a bit closer to the plate. Everyone umpiring these games were instructed to call anything a strike that didn't bounce before the plate, hit the plate, go more than a foot over the batter's head, be more than two feet outside, or hit the batter. Pretty much anything in our area code had to be called strikes, or the games would take days.

THE INCREDIBLE ONE-MAN UMPIRING SHOW

For the seven- and eight-year-old games, we'd ask for a parent volunteer to stand behind the pitcher and umpire the game. Usually, nobody volunteered, as umpiring your child's game is "a lose-lose situation." Calling balls and strikes at this age when pitchers can't throw strikes is impossible. Everyone from the other team thinks you're showing favoritism toward your child's team. Everyone on your child's team, INCLUDING YOUR OWN CHILD, thinks you're trying too hard not to show favoritism toward their team. Everyone on both sides hates the umpire, so usually, no parents volunteer, leaving a coach to do it.

On one rare occasion, I got lucky. Jacob, the dad of one of my players, offered to help. I didn't know him at all. Jacob seemed like a quiet, shy person who brought his son to the games, sat and watched, and supported his son and his team. He was one of the parents I referred to earlier who did his job. He didn't "screw it up" as so many other adults did.

I quickly learned Jacob was anything but quiet and shy. Once he got up from his chair and was on the field, he immediately morphed into someone else. His transformation was like Dr. Banner getting exposed to gamma rays and becoming the Incredible Hulk.

I didn't know if he had any baseball knowledge, but when I started telling him what to do, he looked at me and said authoritatively, "I know what to do." The way he said it sounded more like, "GET OUT OF MY WAY, I'M TAKING OVER NOW!"

The first pitch was about a foot over the batter's head. "STEERIKE ONE!" the no-longer quiet and shy Jacob screamed at an ear-splitting volume.

The second pitch was going to hit the batter, so he fell backward to avoid being hit. "STEERIKE TWO!" Jacob the umpire yelled even louder than the previous pitch.

The third pitch was the best one so far, but it bounced on the plate. "STEERIKE THREE!" Jacob bellowed with an emphatic two-handed punch out sign that would make any seasoned veteran umpire proud.

I went up to him and was going to ask him not to be quite so generous with the strike zone, but he waved me off. "Gotta get 'em swingin'! Gotta move the game along," he told me.

I think what he really meant to say was more like, "OKAY, BUD, THE PARTY'S OVER. THERE'S A NEW SHERIFF IN TOWN AND FROM NOW ON WE'RE DOIN' THINGS MY WAY, YA GOT IT?"

He continued like this for two innings. I don't know if he'd ever umpired before or had secret fantasies about being an umpire, but he was really getting into it. With every pitch, he got louder and louder. Frightened children on a nearby playground ran for their lives. A flock of Canadian geese that were peacefully pooping on the outfield grass packed up their baby geese and flew back to Canada, terrified of this crazy human screaming "STEEERIKE!" at the top of his lungs.

Every pitch was a strike, no matter where it was. Parents watching the game were splitting their sides laughing. In only ten minutes, two full innings were played. It was the fastest two-innings ever played in baseball history. Three up, three down, on both sides for two innings. No runs, no hits, no walks, no base runners, and no errors, for either team.

His strategy worked. He certainly "got 'em swingin'" and "moved the game along." The batters swung at every pitch because they knew everything would be called a strike. They swung at high pitches, low pitches, and everything in between. One kid even swung at a pitch that hit him, but since he swung, it was also a strike.

The final combined box score for two innings for both teams: Thirty-six total pitches thrown, zero balls, thirty-six strikes, zero runs, and zero base runners, all done in only ten minutes! Who says baseball is a slow game?

After two innings, the live pitching ended, and we brought in the pitching machine. Bruce, the other coach, and I went over to thank Jacob for a very memorable evening and to tell him we'll take it from here.

Again, he waved us off. "I'll run the pitching machine," he said. Bruce and I looked at each other, not quite knowing what to do. We were getting concerned. We started with a guy who was quiet and shy, and we'd created a monster.

Jacob was like a man possessed. In no time, he was single-handedly coaching both teams and feeding the pitching machine, while directing batters and fielders. If there was a concession stand, he'd also have been cooking hot dogs and pouring drinks, as well as parking cars and directing traffic in and out of the parking lot! He was "multitasking" before multitasking was even invented!

I said to Bruce, "Hey, why don't I go get us some sandwiches and a couple of beers? We can just sit and watch the game. Our coaching expertise is obviously no longer needed here!"

After the game, we thanked Jacob for his help, and I was afraid he liked it so much he'd want to do it again. But he only attended a few games the rest of the season and didn't offer to help again. Apparently, he gave that game everything he had, and after only one performance of his incredible one-man umpiring show, he was done for the season!

I managed in this league for two seasons while my son was seven and eight. For the most part, games and practices were fun other than dealing with a few obnoxious parents. As crazy as some of those parents were, Jacob and his incredible one-man umpiring show provided more than enough entertainment for two whole seasons of coaching seven- and eight-year-olds.

HOW I BATTED A THOUSAND (LIFETIME CAREER BATTING AVERAGE)

When my son was seven, our town league held a softball game where two teams of coaches played each other to raise money for field improvements. Tickets and food were sold and items donated by local merchants were raffled off. I decided to play even though the last time I played in a softball game was in college, twenty-seven years earlier. From what little I can remember, there was more emphasis during my college softball games on how many beers players could drink in a game than how many runs your team could score.

At forty-eight, I was one of the older coaches, and my skills were rusty. The "coach" of our team ran a pregame team-stretching session hoping to prevent injuries. I've always exercised regularly, and was in good shape, but never stretched quite this much. I stretched and stretched like I had never stretched before. After the stretching session, we practiced catching fly balls in the outfield. It was my turn and a high fly ball was coming down ten feet in front of me. With eyes on the ball, I jogged slowly a few steps straight ahead to get under the ball.

Suddenly, and for no apparent reason, something snapped in the back of my lower right leg. I dropped to the ground like I'd been shot, and the pain was excruciating. My calf muscle was so tight I could barely move my leg. It took a few minutes and two other coaches to help me stand.

Slowly, I got to our bench, obviously unable to play in the game. My whole team of seven- and eight-year-olds came over. Probably three hundred people were there to watch the game, including my whole team. They had come to watch their coach play.

"Coach, what happened, are you going to be able to play? Oh, we hope you can play, we really wanted to see you!" On and on they went! Not wanting to disappoint my players, I had to find a way to play in this game, even if just for an inning.

While my team batted, some guys tried to help me. We put two ice packs on the back of my leg. I spotted a roll of duct tape on the bench. Remembering my dad always saying, "You can fix anything with duct tape," we duct-taped the two ice bags around my leg so they'd stay put. I stood up and was able to walk, but very slowly.

"PUT ME IN COACH, I'M READY TO PLAY!" I yelled to my coach.

"Are you crazy?" he said back to me. "You can barely walk."

"Just let me play first base next inning and then bat once. My team really wants to see their coach play in the game."

"Okay," he said, "but I hope we don't take you home on a stretcher! Your wife won't be happy!"

The next inning, I dragged my right leg out to first base. I looked like a wounded warrior. Unfortunately, nobody took a picture of me, because I must have looked ridiculous playing first base with two ice packs duct-taped to my leg.

Some of the other coaches played regularly in a softball league, were ten years younger than me, and were very good players. I prayed that nobody would hit anything my way, and if I had to catch a throw from another fielder, it had better hit my glove, as I couldn't move at all.

First pitch: grounder to third. *Oh no*, I thought, *He's going to throw me the ball all the way from third and if I have to stretch or reach for the throw, I can't do it.* I found the bag with my foot at the end of my lifeless right leg and squeezed the perfectly thrown frozen rope as it found the pocket of my glove. One out.

The next batter punched one into center field for a single. One on with one out. The next batter hit a hard grounder to short. The second baseman ran toward second. *Oh no, this is even worse*, I thought, *now they're trying to turn two, and I CAN'T be the guy that botches a double play.* As I again found the first base bag with my right foot, the second baseman caught the toss from the shortstop, stepped on second, whirled, and fired a perfect strike to me for the six-four-three double play. AND THE CROWD GOES WILD! Thank God those two guys made great throws to me!

After limping in, I was told I was batting first. As I could barely walk, the other team let me use a pinch runner right from the plate. Having not batted in twenty-seven years, I prayed I'd at least make contact. The first pitch came in and, with a mighty swing, I lifted a lazy flare that just barely made it over the leaping first baseman's glove into short right field. My pinch runner made it to first, and that was not only the end of my game, but the end of my career. One at bat, and one hit. Very impressive! It's now eighteen years later, and I haven't had another at bat since.

There was both good news and bad news. First, the bad news, which I found out the next day. I had torn a calf muscle, probably from too much pregame stretching! It was six months before I walked normally again. The good news was that my players got to see their coach play. I retired from playing with a perfect lifetime batting average of 1.00 (also known as "batting a thousand") for my illustrious career, which ended on the same day it began.

ALL TIME LEADERS FOR CAREER BATTING AVERAGE

RANKING	PLAYER	LIFETIME BATTING AVERAGE
1.)	RANDY CORWIN	1.00
2.)	TY COBB	.366
3.)	TRIS SPEAKER	.345
4.)	TED WILLIAMS	.344
5.)	BABE RUTH	.342
6.)	LOU GEHRIG	.340
7.)	TONY GWYNN	.338
8.)	STAN MUSIAL	.331

COACHING NINE- AND TEN-YEAR-OLDS

I coached in this league for two years. As a manager in the first year, I got fed up with coaches who cared about nothing but winning. They didn't care if the kids had fun or learned anything. Some would do anything to win. It drove me crazy, and after the season ended, I let league officials and all coaches know that kids were being sent the wrong message by the way some coaches conducted themselves. Making my feelings known cost me the chance to ever manage in the spring league again.

In this nine- and ten-year-old age group, it was beginning to resemble real baseball. You could steal bases, with limitations. Actual umpires were used, rather than a parent volunteer. The players were older, could reach the plate from the mound, and some pitchers could throw strikes on a semi-regular basis.

In this league, unlike the lower levels, wins and losses were tracked. Some coaches checked the standings of who was in first place or last place daily, if not hourly. Even though winning was not supposed to be the priority and coaches were supposed to fairly divide playing time between stars and misfits, this didn't always happen. Not all coaches went to great lengths like I did to get everyone involved and make the games fun. Some did whatever they could get away with to win, which irritated me to no end — and this nonsense went on all season.

Certain coaches would only let their best players pitch, catch, and play first base, rather than giving others a chance. The stars played every inning of every game, while weaker players sat on the bench half the game.

My son played a second season in this league, which we called "AAA," when he was ten, and I was an assistant coach for the first time. He was becoming a decent catcher and pitcher. He was one of the best pitchers in his age group, not overpowering, but threw strikes, rarely walking batters. He was frequently used as a "closer" in the final inning if we were leading to finish games. Nolan, one of his teammates, nicknamed him "Pap," like the Boston closer at the time, Jonathon Papelbon.

We had a fun season, and although we didn't come close to winning the championship, we went to the semi-final game of a multi-town weekend tournament. There were several dozen teams for players from nine to twelve. The regular spring teams were used, but unlike the supposedly "recreational" attitude of the spring league, this was a competitive tournament, and the goal was to win. In the regular spring league, it supposedly wasn't "all about winning," but here it was. All weekend, coaches screamed at umpires, and those coaches who were "out for blood" were absolutely in their glory.

"I'M MAD AS HELL, AND I'M NOT GOING TO TAKE IT ANYMORE!"

This line from the 1976 movie *Network* summed up how I felt after my first season coaching nine- and ten-year-olds. It was a frustrating season. The team I selected in the draft got torn up, and I ended up being forced to replace three players I really liked with three players I didn't want any part of. The three players forced on me were annoying jerks who never listened to their coaches, didn't get along with teammates, and had obnoxious parents.

All season long, I watched coaches in what was supposedly a recreational league doing anything to win, coaching like their next meal depended on winning. Coaches pushed the boundaries on rules and argued with umpires constantly. Coaches lied about pitch counts, had pitchers "quick pitch" at times, and had stars play every inning while lesser players rode the bench.

Winning was not supposed to be the top priority, but it absolutely was. Coaches screamed at players for making errors. I saw coaches pull players off the field and sit them on the bench in the middle of an inning for dropping a fly ball or booting a grounder. Two coaches had a heated argument during a game, which almost turned into a fight before cooler heads jumped in to separate them.

A lot of collective situations piling up during the season had me completely fed up with coaches "pulling out all the stops" like every game was game seven of the world championship. What was supposed to be an atmosphere of good sportsmanship and friendly competition had become a cutthroat, win-at-all-costs mentality. I was tired of constantly watching grown-ups screw it up. I kept wondering why all this nonsense was necessary. To give you a better chance to win a nine- or ten-year-old's baseball game?

Six decades ago, George Jetson showed us futuristic technology and amazing inventions that we laughed at, but they all happened. We've made incredible advances in medicine, science, and technology. Why can't we make similar advances in how adults behave in youth baseball games? In this day and age, aren't we smarter than that? Aren't we better than that?

Unfortunately, we're not. I couldn't take it any longer and told the top brass running the league that they needed to address the problem of overly competitive coaches right away. It was the end of the regular spring season and playoffs had begun. They assured me they would address the problem of poor sportsmanship and coaches doing whatever it took to win.

HOW THE LEAGUE ADDRESSED THE PROBLEM

The spring playoffs were underway, and my team, which wasn't very good, lost in the first round. There were a few playoff rules that were a bit unclear, so before playoffs continued, an email was sent by the league to coaches with rule clarifications. I assumed the email would also include reminders about showing good sportsmanship and toning down the excessive competitiveness. I was outraged after reading the email that none of my concerns were mentioned.

That was it. All they did was clarify a few rules. Not a single word was said about overly competitive coaches doing whatever it took to win in a recreational league. I was now past my boiling point. I was mad as hell and was not going to take it anymore. Regrettably, I made a terrible decision, taking matters into my own hands.

HOW I ADDRESSED THE PROBLEM

It wasn't any one incident that pushed me to do something I shouldn't have; it was a series of episodes, one after another. They never stopped. The league's failure to do anything about it was, for me, "the straw that broke the camel's back."

Since the league didn't address the problem, I did, which was a mistake. All season long, I watched coaches who were way too driven to win in a recreational league. I was sick of it, was angry, and reacted inappropriately—a decision I regretted then, and still regret today.

Some might wonder if I was so frustrated with the way things were being done, why didn't I just quit, walk away, and let somebody else deal with this insanity? Maybe I was young and naive, thinking I could change things, and make it better for the kids. I cared, and for that, I was punished, but I felt the league left me no other choice to get my message across.

I fired off a strongly worded email to managers, coaches, and board members. It was about how disappointed I was with some coaches in what was supposed to be a recreational league being so consumed with winning, and how this mind-set sends kids the wrong message. It was well written, with no names mentioned, and no inappropriate language. Although I knew some people might not like what I had to say, my message was long overdue.

I shouldn't have sent the email, but I did, knowing there may be consequences. I spent a half hour writing the email, and twice that long deciding if I should send it. I knew after I clicked "send," the s--t was going to hit the fan. After hovering over the "send" box for about an hour, I closed my eyes, said a prayer, and clicked "send."

And yes, the s--t hit the fan.

I got many replies. Reactions varied widely. Some supported me saying, "It's about time somebody said something about all the nonsense going on in a recreational league. Thank you for having the guts to do it!" Others wanted to have me publicly tarred, feathered, and flogged!

The most interesting response came from the board of directors. Their response was no response. Complete radio silence. Not a word from anyone. The season was over for me. I put it behind me and hoped what I said might wake some people up and next year things would be better. Wishful thinking!

MY BANISHMENT

I'd managed for four straight seasons and planned to do it again the next year. Since I'd managed that long, and players and parents liked me, I thought it was just a formality waiting for the manager selections for the next season to be announced.

The next spring, when the league's list of managers was announced, I wasn't on the list. I was at first stunned, before realizing this was the response from the board of directors to my infamous email.

I was unofficially "blacklisted." They would never let me manage in the spring league again. That was their response.

I was shocked, but not surprised. I had stirred the pot, upset the applecart, rocked the boat, and whatever other expressions describe challenging the status quo. I was found guilty of all charges, and the judge, jury, and executioner, without saying a word to me, handed down my sentence.

I had been banished. This was the worst possible punishment for someone who loves baseball as much as I do and loved even more spending so much great time with my son and a bunch of kids while running a team. I was devastated. I was banished from coaching for speaking out against coaches who were far too competitive in what was supposedly a recreational league. Does that make any sense?

I had rocked the "Good Ship Lollipop," and the captain threw me overboard. Many coaches and parents were shocked I wasn't managing, as I'd been a fixture of the league for years. Fortunately, the manager who drafted my son for his final year in the nine-and-ten league needed an assistant, and we worked well together. It was a fun year, and being an assistant coach instead of a manager for the first time was a lot less work.

ELEVEN- AND TWELVE-YEAR-OLDS

As I was no longer a team manager, I was hoping that whoever drafted my eleven-year-old son would take me on as an assistant coach. I offered to help his new manager as an assistant coach and was turned down because he already had three assistant coaches.

As a "youth baseball lifer," I was going stir-crazy just sitting and watching, and decided to explore the possibility of umpiring, which I was always interested in. I took local umpire training classes, mostly attended by teenagers. I eventually wound up teaching these classes and running our local youth umpiring program for about ten years. I umpired about twenty games that season for my town but, for obvious reasons, wasn't allowed to umpire my son's games, except for once.

Before the games started that season, my son's team had scrimmages with another team just to give both teams some practice in a game-type situation. My son's manager, knowing that I was now umpiring, asked if I could umpire the scrimmage. Normally, nobody umpires a game that a family member is playing in, but since it was only a scrimmage, no big deal, right?

WRONG! Everybody on the opposing team knew my son was on the other team and thought my strike zone was biased toward him and his team. Everyone on my son's team thought I was trying too hard to look like my strike zone was unbiased and thought that I was favoring their opponent.

And remember, this was just a "MEANINGLESS SCRIMMAGE"!

I umpired a bunch of local games that season and found that umpiring was a completely different side of baseball—plus, unlike coaching, you got paid for umpiring! After that season ended, I took classes to become a state-certified umpire. I could then work more games, at any level, from nine-year-olds through high school and legion games.

Although I had shifted my focus from coaching to umpiring, I surprisingly got one last chance to manage a team when my son was eleven.

THE ELEVEN-YEAR-OLD SUMMER TRAVEL TEAM

Since I'd been "banished" from managing in the spring rec league, I threw my hat in the ring and expressed interest in managing the summer all-star travel team of eleven-year-olds.

I endured multiple interviews, feeling like I was applying for a job with high-level security clearance for the FBI or CIA. After being intensely grilled by a six-person selection committee, I was offered the job but was warned the team probably wouldn't be very good, and some parents of players on the team were tough to deal with. I knew them all. They were highly competitive people who thought winning youth baseball games was the number one priority in life.

My kind of people!

They were delusional about how good their sons' baseball skills were. I'd seen them play, and they were decent, but that's all they were.

The coach who ran the team the year before, when the same group was ten, was not returning. His team didn't do well, and I figured I couldn't do much worse. It was mostly the same players returning as eleven-year-olds.

The twelve players on the team were all good, but only

three were real "all stars." The other nine could have been chosen from twenty players who all had their strengths and weaknesses, like my son. Having a smaller population than other towns in the league, only twenty-four players even tried out for the team. Larger towns in the league had over one hundred players try out, so it was unlikely we'd be as strong a team as more populated towns could put together.

My son was a pretty good pitcher and first baseman, but not a great hitter. He understood that, on this team, he'd probably be more of a role player than a starter. On our team, everyone was a fairly good player, but being fairly good simply wasn't good enough in this bloodthirsty, cut-throat, win-at-all-costs league.

Some parents of my players were upset that we weren't winning. They blamed me, even though it was their kid throwing wild pitches, booting grounders, dropping fly balls, or striking out on pitches in the dirt. They blamed me, but none of them stepped up to help! They were just card-carrying members of "the complainers club."

In this twelve-town competitive league, the goal was to win. Some managers and coaches, as expected, went nuts as far as "taking things way too seriously." Of our eleven losses, five were more like massacres, "mercy rule" short-ened games ending after only four innings because we trailed by ten or more runs.

We only won three games, but one of those three wins was particularly satisfying—not just to me but to my players and even the managers of every other team in the league.

It was the final game of the summer season. We missed the playoffs because only the top eight teams made the playoffs, and we finished tenth. At least we weren't last!

Our opponent in game fourteen was undefeated and expected to destroy us just by showing up. They were the best team in the league. Although all teams in the league respected them for their skills, they were disliked by everyone. Their coaches, especially the manager, argued about everything that didn't go their way, and the players conducted themselves like their coaches did. The players acted like spoiled rotten, entitled bullies. They all knew they were very good and were full of themselves, showing no sportsmanship to opposing players or respect for umpires.

Despite being a highly unlikeable team, they were outstanding baseball players. Obliterating their first few opponents like they were playing against seven-year-olds, it was expected just a few games into the season they would go undefeated and win the championship.

When they arrived at our field, I introduced myself to their universally disliked manager and quickly found out why everyone around the league felt this way. After a minute of small talk, the manager put his arm around me and said, "I know you guys have only won two games and you probably know we're undefeated. It's very important for us to complete a perfect season, so I just want to let you know that we will not be taking it easy on you guys just because this game means nothing in the standings."

Although a bit surprised by his rather brash proclamation of their intent to destroy us, I just said something back to him like, "Sounds good, let's play."

I went back to our dugout shaking my head and called the players over. I repeated what their manager had just said to me. "What a jerk," said Nolan, our best player, who turned to the others and said, "Guys, I know they're good, but wouldn't it be cool if we could be the ones who ruin their perfect season?"

These guys obviously thought that they'd blow us off the map without breaking a sweat. They didn't take us seriously, and played their worst game of the season, dropping fly balls, booting grounders, making poor throws, and walking batters. Meanwhile, my guys played way over their heads. We had timely hitting, fabulous defense, and some very lucky bounces when we really needed them!

Gary, our starting pitcher, pitched four solid innings, but we were down by two runs. In the bottom of the fourth inning, Nolan belted a three-run homer to change the score from us trailing 4-2, to leading 5-4. Michael, our pitcher in the fifth inning, was shaky, loading the bases with nobody out, but the baseball gods had our backs! With bases full, and nobody out, a hard grounder up the middle bounced off the pitching rubber, changed direction, and hit the runner from first on his way to second. That gave us an out, and the ball was dead when it hit the runner so no other runners could advance, costing them two runs. The next batter scorched a low-line drive, but Nolan made a great diving catch and landed on third base to double up the runner on third who was off on contact! Three outs!

I don't think our opponent had ever trailed in a game all season, and they couldn't handle it. I saw them unraveling. Their manager was riding the umpires and yelling at his assistant coaches. The players were screaming at each other once we took the lead.

Their manager was one of those guys who, if things didn't go well, blamed everything on the umpires. We couldn't add to our lead in the bottom of the fifth, but he kept chirping to the umpires, and even shouted to me in the fifth inning,

"Where did you find these umpires that don't have a clue what they're doing?"

I couldn't believe the umpires didn't toss this clown, especially after that last remark. Maybe since he was such a jerk, they wanted him there to see his "perfect season" go up in flames as much as we did! The "clueless umpires" seemed like they were doing fine to me.

Before the sixth inning started, he approached the plate umpire. I assumed he wanted to apologize for his remarks the inning before. Another incorrect assumption on my part! Instead, he asked, "Why are you calling nothing but strikes for their pitchers, and nothing but balls for my pitchers?"

"It's a simple explanation, coach. Their pitchers are throwing strikes, and yours are not!"

I liked that explanation! Why mince words when you don't have to? If I was the umpire, I would've ejected this guy three times by now, but these umpires chose to just ignore him.

My son, Dan, for the past couple of years, had been a very good "short outing" relief pitcher. As a ten-year-old, we often used him as a "closer" to pitch one strong final inning, preserve the lead, and end the game. He had a closer's mentality, meaning he pitched his best if he started the inning with no runners already on base, and we were leading. Nolan was his teammate last year who had nicknamed him "Pap."

Our summer team rarely had a lead for him to try to close a game, but this time we did! As Dan warmed up before the top of the sixth, Nolan, our third baseman, yelled to him, "C'mon, Pap, finish them off and let's go home! Just like you did all last year!"

"Pap" grinned and nodded to his teammate.

Dan didn't throw as hard as other pitchers, but he was very accurate, and could hit any spot where the catcher held his mitt. I had the catcher give him knee-high targets on the inside corner. He'd get a lot of called strikes, and even if the batter hit the ball, it wouldn't be hit very hard.

First pitch: called strike at the knees.

Second pitch: batter gets jammed and hits a soft popup to second. One out!

Next batter: called strike, knee high, inside corner. The manager was screaming at the umpire. "C'mon, it practically hit him!"

Next pitch: same spot and a weak grounder back to the mound. Easy underhand toss to first. Two outs!

I think the manager would've been tossing chairs by now if there were any chairs around to toss. His perfect season was one out away from being ruined by a team with two wins and eleven losses!

Next pitch: called strike, again on the inside corner at the knees.

Second pitch: same spot, a defensive swing fouled off. With a count of 0-2, I saw the batter back way off the plate, obviously expecting another pitch on the inside corner six inches from his knees. Our catcher saw it too, and at the last second, positioned his glove for the first time knee high, but on the "OUTSIDE CORNER" of the plate. The stunned batter froze, as the pitch hit the mitt perfectly.

"Steerike three!" screamed the umpire.

I never reacted this way but was so happy to have spoiled the "perfect season" of this idiot whose life revolved around winning youth baseball games. I ran out to the mound and bear-hugged my eleven-year-old son, who for one last time in his life, enjoyed the thrill of being "Pap" and closing out the win for his team.

"C'mon, Dad, you're embarrassing me," he said and laughed, while trying to squirm out of my grip. Because these guys were such jerks, spoiling their perfect season made everyone on the team feel like champions. I quickly had everyone line up for the customary post-game handshake with the other team.

When you shake hands, high five, or do a fist pump with your opponent after a game, everyone's expected to show good sportsmanship, whether you win or lose, and say something like, "Hey, guys, great game."

Instead, this buffoon says to me, "I want to see the league certification papers for those umpires." He was one of those coaches that, when things go wrong, it was never his fault. Just blame it all on the umpires.

I wasn't even sure such documents existed but assured him that our league director would send that to him. I asked our league director about his request, and his response was something like: "F--k him, he's an a--hole and everybody in the league can't stand him. I'm sure every team in the league will be thanking you for beating them."

He was right. For the next two days, I got emails and phone calls from every manager in the league congratulating and thanking us for beating this universally disliked team. With only three wins, our season wasn't exactly perfect, but because we played the "spoiler," neither was theirs! The following week they had three playoff wins to clinch the championship. I didn't call to congratulate them.

That was my last managing job, which ended on a very high note. Despite finishing with a dismal record of three wins and eleven losses, the players did their best, winning as a team, losing as a team, and having fun as a team. In my mind, especially at this age, having fun is more important than how many games you win. Remember: BASEBALL IS SUPPOSED TO BE FUN!

A SATIRICAL LOOK AT HOW TYPICAL YOUTH BASEBALL LEAGUES ARE RUN

Baseball is supposedly a simple kid's game, but to run a league to play this simple kid's game, complex bureaucracies are formed like those of large corporations. When bureaucracies exist, getting anything done becomes an ordeal.

The board of directors consists of elected officers and positions appointed by the elected officials. Being a "board member"—such as president, commissioner, secretary, treasurer, league director, umpire-in-chief, equipment manager, etc.—takes a lot of time and these are all unpaid volunteer positions.

At times during the season, these volunteer positions are as time-consuming as full-time jobs. It's not easy to find people to do these jobs. People running leagues put in long hours and spend a lot of time together, forming strong friendships and "political cliques." I said it before, and I'll say it again: What could politics possibly **NOT SCREW UP?**

THE MISSION STATEMENT

Step one to complicate a simple kid's game is to come up with a "mission statement," a long, drawn-out sentence describing exactly what, as an organization, you want to accomplish. You can't just state the obvious like, "We want to give our kids a place to play baseball. That's too simple and not how things are done. You must come up with something more creative, such as:

"Our mission is to provide the young athletes of our town with a program of learning and playing the game of baseball in an atmosphere conducive to friendly competition, safety, good sportsmanship, and fair play, with an opportunity to grow as a player and member of our community."

Of course, coming up with a mission statement requires meetings where you form a subcommittee whose "mission" seems to be to hold meeting after meeting. Ultimately, the subcommittee will come up with a very long-winded mission statement like the one above that no one could possibly care less about.

Can't we keep it simple? Is a mission statement really necessary? We're not running a multibillion-dollar company that employs thousands of people worldwide. We're just forming a program so kids can play baseball.

If a more official-sounding mission statement is needed,

MAYFIELD YOUTH BASEBALL MISSION STATEMENT

OUR MISSION IS TO TAKE A SIMPLE KID'S GAME
AND
MAKE IT AS COMPLICATED AS HUMANLY POSSIBLE.

that longer version isn't bad but doesn't tell the whole story. It should really be more like this:

> "Our mission is to take baseball, a simple kid's game, and create a highly structured, insanely complicated program with countless rules, ridiculous regulations, absurd bylaws, statutes, limitations, and restrictions upon restrictions, all administered and governed by multilayered political bureaucracies, in order to achieve our ultimate goal of making a simple kid's game as complex as humanly possible."

I really like that one, but the subcommittee might not agree with me.

THE MONTHLY BOARD MEETINGS

Nobody complicates simple things like people running youth sports programs. Baseball might only be played for three or four months, but meetings are held all year. Discussions are held on anything from field improvements to what fees to charge to play baseball, etc.

Hundreds of families have kids in baseball, and everyone is encouraged to help, but it's the same ten or fifteen people that come to meetings. Other parents don't bother, claiming they're too busy. Some of these "too busy" parents are the "complainers" mentioned earlier. They're always the last ones to offer to help but the first to complain about what everyone else does.

Although I had managed teams for several years, I had no interest in helping run the league. It took enough time just to run a team. Complaints about monthly meetings aren't unfounded. Meetings are very formally run, and sometimes go on for hours. Consequently, I never attended meetings, as I figured I'd end up getting roped into doing something else I didn't have time for.

I was not alone. Attendance at meetings was at an all-time low. The only people that showed up once were the commissioner, president, secretary, and treasurer. The commissioner issued a "mandate" to coaches that anyone not attending meetings regularly will not be coaching anymore. Reluctantly, I began going to meetings.

My first baseball meeting seemed more like a stockholders' meeting of a Fortune 500 company. In a large meeting room in the town library, the commissioner runs things from a table in front. He's flanked by his president, vice president, secretary, and treasurer. Everyone else sits facing these high-ranking board members in front of them.

"I'd like a motion from the floor to begin the meeting," the commissioner stated. Somebody raised his hand. "Okay, we have a motion from Pete to begin the meeting. Thank you, Pete. Can we have a second?" Somebody else raises his hand. "Thank you, Fred, for the second to begin the meeting. All in favor, please raise your hands." Hands are raised, and he said, "Okay the vote is unanimous, so let's start the meeting."

I was thinking, can't he just say, "Hi, guys, let's get started"? Instead, we've wasted ten minutes doing all this procedural nonsense. If it's this complicated to just start a meeting, imagine what it takes to resolve a real issue, like setting up teams fairly so one team isn't winning every game, while other teams get destroyed every game.

Something like this requires forming a "subcommittee" which I once served on to remedy this very issue.

Four of us met twice a week for two weeks, eight hours in total. We had good ideas that were all shot down in five minutes at the next meeting: "Nah, the draft works great, we'll stay with that," was what the board concluded after we gave up eight hours of our lives that we'll never get back. (Sorry for the digression.)

Back to the meeting. After the meeting had finally, officially started, the head guy said, "Let's begin the meeting by hearing the secretary's report with the minutes from our last meeting."

The secretary stood up, cleared his throat, and started with, "Our last meeting began at approximately 7:02 p.m., eastern standard time on Tuesday, February 4, with the following fourteen people in attendance . . ."

After droning on and on for about ten minutes, he mercifully finished. Every last detail of the previous meeting was reviewed.

I'm not sure, but it wouldn't even surprise me if his highly detailed minutes of last month's meeting included something like:

"At approximately 7:47 p.m., eastern standard time, the meeting was briefly interrupted when Sam Quagmire sneezed. Paul Periwinkle turned and said to Sam Quagmire, 'God bless you, Sam.' Sam Quagmire then said, 'Thank you,' to Paul Periwinkle, and at approximately 7:48 p.m., eastern standard time, the meeting resumed."

I didn't remember a word he said about the previous meeting and doubt anyone else did either.

After more than two hours of riveting discussion, the meeting ended. Closing the meeting was as complicated as starting it, but when the commissioner asked for a motion to end the meeting, everyone's hand shot up. When he asked for a "second" to end the meeting, everyone raised both hands. Apparently, I wasn't the only one whose brain was cooked and just wanted to get out of there.

I guess we covered what was needed. I couldn't recall much but wasn't concerned. In the unlikely event I missed something important, the next meeting would start by rehashing every bloody detail from the prior meeting, which everyone forgot because they were all zoned out too!

Good thing I have plenty of time to waste! And they wonder why nobody goes to those meetings!

FAST TRACK TO THE TOP OF THE FOOD CHAIN

Occasionally, something funny happens at a meeting. Sometimes, a new parent of a player would show up and offer to do something the league might need help with.

Since there usually weren't many people at meetings, if anyone new came, we'd start by having everyone introduce themselves and say if they were a coach, treasurer, parent of a nine-year-old, etc.

Once a new parent came to his first meeting. "Nick" had a five-year-old who was going to play T-ball the following spring, and he wanted to manage his son's team.

"Excellent!" said the commissioner. "Great to have new people joining us! Before we go on, let's have a vote to elect Nick as manager of his son's T-ball team. All in favor, raise your hands."

Everyone's hands shot up. "Congratulations, Nick, you are now a T-ball manager. Thank you!" No wasted time here on this important issue!

As part of this meeting, the board was also filling positions for the upcoming season, such as directors of the various age groups, fundraising chairman, secretary, president of the league, etc.

A position for director of the T-ball division was available, and when this opening was brought up, Nick raised his hand and said, "Since I'm going to manage my son's T-ball team, why don't I do that too?"

"All in favor? Say 'aye'!" said the commissioner. The vote was unanimous. This new, young "up-and-comer" was climbing the corporate ladder right before our very eyes.

Ten minutes later, the commissioner asked for nominations for league president, the number two position running the league. It's a very time-consuming job that's often tough to fill. There were no volunteers.

"This is a problem if we can't get someone," said the commissioner. Nick raised his hand again and asked, "Exactly what does the president do?" After about five minutes of listening to the commissioner recite the duties of the president, Nick stated, "I can do that."

Pleasantly surprised and also shocked, before Nick changed his mind, the commissioner immediately called for a vote to elect Nick the new league president. The vote was again unanimous.

Nick went from being an undrafted rookie free agent and unknown parent to manager of T-ball, to director of T-ball, to league president, all in under twenty minutes! Who says baseball is a slow game? Nothing like the fast track to the top!

THE OPENING DAY FESTIVITIES

This great annual event known as "opening day" can be fun but tops the list of turning something easy into a monumental project. Opening day happens in mid- to late-April, but in New England, opening day signifies much more than just the start of another baseball season. In the northeast, it's a celebration of spring. It means the long, cold winter months are finally in the rearview mirror. The snow is gone. The grass is turning green. Bare trees have leaves again. Cars aren't covered in salt and sand like they are all winter. The sun is stronger. The temperature is rising. Winter coats go away, and short-sleeve shirts triumphantly return. Birds are chirping, people are happier, and best of all, BASEBALL IS BACK!

While you could just start playing games, THAT'S WAY TOO SIMPLE and completely contradicts the mission statement, which, I remind you, is to take something simple and make it complicated. What starts out as "Let's invite the whole league, and we'll do a few speeches to thank everybody before the first game" turns into an event rivaling a royal wedding.

Some communities hold massive opening-day ceremonies, which require planning, organizing task forces, and forming subcommittees. Food and drinks need to be purchased, grills and tents are rented, police details arranged, photographers booked, etc. The process starts almost as soon as the previous season ends. It takes many people a ton of time and effort to organize this, and we all know what brings May flowers. Every few years, an uninvited April shower shows up on opening day, and everything's called off, sometimes at the last minute. With so many moving parts, this can't be rescheduled, and hundreds of hours spent planning this massive event goes down the drain along with all the pummeling water cascading from the heavens.

Assuming the weather does cooperate, a parade route is planned, ending at the baseball field where the first game of the season is played. Every team in the league marches in the parade, in full uniform, from five-year-old T-ballers to the big kids, the twelve-year-olds, along with managers, coaches, and league organizers.

Of course, what's a parade without police cars and fire trucks, lights flashing, horns and sirens blaring, rolling slowly through town? You feel bad for any poor souls stuck at an intersection for twenty minutes while the parade goes through. Hope nobody's in a hurry to get somewhere! It's fun for the five- and six-year-olds, but after doing it six times, the twelve-year-olds probably think it's pretty lame and would rather be home playing video games. Parents line the streets of the parade route and wave as their team passes by.

Once at the field, teams sit on the outfield grass while the crowd gathers around the perimeter of the field. The top brass of the league makes long-winded speeches thanking everyone for their hard work. The players couldn't care less about speeches, and most people can't hear them anyway because the PA system never seems to work.

After those speeches, usually a town official, state representative, or other politician, makes another dopey speech that nobody can hear. Following that snooze fest is the singing of the national anthem by a local kid from a church choir or school chorus. Half the time, they are so nervous doing this in front of hundreds of people, that even if they manage to remember the words, their rendition is usually not a Whitney Houston–like performance.

After that, the grand finale is to throw out the ceremonial "first pitch." I find this hilarious, as whoever does this NEVER knows how to throw a ball. On a small diamond, the distance from the mound to the plate is forty-six feet. Usually, the person who does this stands halfway between the mound and the plate, throws the ball about eight feet, leaving it to bounce and roll the rest of the way to the catcher. Not very impressive. You'd think someone asked to do this honor would practice their throwing a few days before so they don't completely embarrass themselves, but they never do!

After that, a group of five-year-old T-ballers are handed the microphone and scream the words that everyone's been waiting for:

"PLAY BALL!"

At last, another season has begun of kids playing baseball games and adults taking the games way too seriously. Let the shenanigans begin!

TEAM PICTURES

On opening day, players have individual and team pictures taken. Parents can buy team pictures and pictures of their child swinging a bat or throwing a ball. You can order small pictures, big pictures, and even baseball cards. My son is now twenty-five and the collection of pictures from when he was five through twelve have never left the drawer we shoved them in the day they arrived in the mail. The baseball cards he planned to trade with friends fifteen years ago are still in the wrapper. Nice gig for the photographer, but my advice to parents: "SAVE YOUR MONEY!"

TRYOUTS, A.K.A. "THE LOST WEEKEND"

The biggest complaint by parents, and not just "the complainers," is teams are not fairly constructed. There's always a team that wins almost every game, while another loses almost every game. The goal of the league is to create parity. In a perfect youth baseball world, everyone should have a .500 record, but it never happens, and it never will, no matter how hard leagues try to create balanced teams.

In a futile attempt to divide the talent equally, a lengthy and complicated draft process is held to pick teams. Before the draft, all players must be evaluated through a long, arduous process. Although there are no cuts, it's known as "tryouts" and is held in February at an indoor baseball facility.

Team managers watch players throw, pitch, catch, bat, and do some fielding. It takes about ten minutes per player for this, so if you have eighty kids to evaluate, it may take eight hours or more to evaluate everyone. This is usually split into two sessions on a Saturday and Sunday. I refer to this as "the Lost Weekend."

While you pay close attention to the first few players, taking extensive notes, by the time you reach the twentieth player, you've become numb, both body and brain. Some kids you know and some you don't. Shortly, your mind is somewhere else. To a casual observer, you look like you're watching, but your thorough notes at the beginning become meaningless doodles by the end.

After surviving the Lost Weekend, managers assemble useful notes from the beginning of tryouts, along with meaningless doodles from later when their minds were elsewhere. With this information, they decide who's good, who's mediocre, and who doesn't know which end of the bat to hold. Soon, the big night arrives: "Draft Night"!

THE DRAFT, A.K.A. "THE LOST WEEKNIGHT"

Draft Night is big. REALLY BIG! For some managers, this is clearly the biggest event of their year, possibly their lives. From the recent Lost Weekend, managers have meaningful notes from early in tryouts when they were actually paying attention and meaningless doodles from later in tryouts when they weren't. Managers also get evaluations from the player's previous manager, where players are rated from one to five on how they hit, run, catch, pitch, and throw. It's just an opinion of their previous coach, the value of which is questionable at best.

I affectionately refer to Draft Night, which takes three to four grueling hours, as "the Lost Weeknight."

In summary, Draft Night managers are armed with the following material:

1. Memories of kids you've coached before, which may or may not still be relevant.
2. Meaningful notes from when you were actually awake during the Lost Weekend.
3. Meaningless doodles from when you were snoozing during the Lost Weekend.

4. Potentially useless evaluations from managers you probably think are morons.
5. Managers are now ready to step into the "WAR ROOM"!

For my first draft, I brought with me a few scribbled notes that were stuffed in a folder, a broken pencil, and a pen that was out of ink. Other managers had laptops. Obviously, they were far more prepared than I was. I thought, as I often do, *Is all this really necessary? It's just a bunch of kids playing baseball.* Then, I quickly reminded myself of our mission statement, which as we all know, is to take something simple and make it as complicated as possible.

Although there is a draft in pro baseball, it doesn't get the coverage of the pro football draft. Having a recreational baseball league hold a lengthy, complicated draft like the pros do is crazy. Except for not having TV coverage, many youth league drafts run the same way. When it's your turn to choose a player, the announcement is made: "Coach Collins, your team is now on the clock. You have five minutes to make your selection!" And the stopwatch has started! Four minutes and fifty-nine agonizing seconds later, Coach Collins hands his selection in. The announcement is then made: "With the twenty-third overall pick in this year's draft, Coach Collins of the Sun Rays has selected Andrew McGillicuddy, so let's remove Andrew McGillicuddy from the board. Next up, with the twenty-fourth overall pick in the draft, is Coach Harper of the Crushers. Coach Harper, you are now on the clock. You have five minutes to make your selection!" And the stopwatch has started again, so it's easy to see how this process takes FOREVER!

A tension-filled, emotionally charged, highly complex

method of picking teams, which takes way too long, makes perfect sense.

It seems that if people running youth baseball leagues have two ways to do anything—one being simple and the other being difficult—the decision is easy: You ALWAYS, and without hesitation, choose the hard way. Spending three to four hours to divide up one hundred players into eight teams with the goal of teams being somewhat equal is a pipe dream. IT WON'T HAPPEN, for these reasons:

1. Every manager secretly wants to have the best team and win. Nobody really wants to have eight equal teams, even if they publicly say they do.
2. Whoever gets the best player is already better than everyone else. And if two or three of the best players land on the same team, don't even bother playing games. Just hand them the trophy and spare everyone else the agony of getting crushed by the "stacked team."
3. Whoever gets stuck with the worst players who strike out every time and make errors whenever the ball is hit to them is running in quicksand. Their team is finished before the season even starts!
4. No matter what lengths you go to choose balanced teams, there will always be one team winning almost every game, and others losing almost every game.

I'm certain you can pick one hundred names out of a hat in fifteen minutes. This will probably yield teams no more unequally balanced than you get by running a tension-filled three-to-four-hour draft. Keep in mind that the three-to-four-hour draft (the Lost Weeknight) comes right after the ten-to-twelve-hour Lost Weekend of tryouts, which everyone is still recuperating from. That's a ton of time to spend on a process that really doesn't work!

To start the festivities, the commissioner has managers pick numbers from a hat to determine the draft order in each round.

When a manager chooses players early in the draft, this is what to look for:

1. Is he a decent player? Can he catch, hit, run, throw, pitch, etc.?
2. Is he a nice kid, a "team player," or a jerk you don't want on your team?
3. Is he "coachable"? Meaning will he listen to you and try to learn?

In later stages of the draft, what you look for once all the good players are gone changes. Now you try to avoid players who are so bad that your team's much better when they don't show up. When picking toward the end of a draft, this is what you look for:

1. Can this player EVER field a ball hit his way?
2. Can this player EVER catch a ball that another player throws to him?
3. Can this player EVER get on base, or is he an "automatic out" every time?

One year, at the end of a marathon three-hour draft session, one of the four worst remaining players had to be chosen by Coach Bill. Everybody was pretty tired and some of the coaches were getting a bit silly and punchy but tried to keep focused on finishing up. Bill said to his fellow coaches, "Guys, help me out, I have no idea which bad player to take. Anybody have any suggestions?"

Upon hearing Bill's request for help, Coach Gene piped up jokingly, "C'mon already, Bill, just pick somebody so we can get out of here before midnight. Since the four kids left all stink, why don't you just take whoever has the best-looking mom? Can any of you guys provide Bill with some intel on that?"

PLEASE, MOMS, DON'T BE OFFENDED BY THAT. IT WAS JUST A JOKE!

It was a funny suggestion at the time, but not generally considered a great strategy when putting together a baseball team.

The goal was to have all teams finish with .500 records. The problem is there are usually only a few real "impact" players, and the team which drafts them will be good. While you'd like all teams to be equal, if there are only three impact players and eight teams, the teams will be unbalanced no matter how many hours or days you spend on player evaluations and drafts.

One year, by luck of the draw, I got the number one pick in the draft, and there was one player every coach wanted. Jack was by far the best player in the league, so I chose him. On and on we went, and three grueling hours later, the eight teams were picked.

Then the whining began! It sounded like a bunch of spoiled-rotten six-year-olds who were told they couldn't have dessert until after they ate their vegetables.

"I've got no pitching," proclaimed one.

"All the good hitters are on his team," pointed out another.

"My team will lose every game, and his team will win every game," moaned a third.

On and on the complaints went, until the league president jumped in and said, "Okay, let's tweak it a little bit."

With my number one pick, and several other good players, I had a very strong team, which everybody knew and whined about nonstop. ANOTHER hour later, after the draft was "tweaked a little bit," I had to swap my best player in the league to another team for not just one, but two really bad players, as well as a third player that never listened to anything I said. None of these three players got along well with the rest of the team and, to make matters worse, they all had obnoxious parents!

All I know is that my once-strong team, after we "tweaked it a little bit," finished the season with three wins and thirteen losses that year. The team getting my best player for their two misfits had fifteen wins, only one loss, and won the championship. Instead of spending entire weekends on tryouts, in addition to evaluations, meetings, and a four-hour draft, couldn't we have pulled names out of a hat and formed teams that were just as unbalanced in about fifteen minutes?

We could've, but that would have been way too simple. Remember that when there's a choice of achieving similar results by doing something the easy way or doing it the hard way, you MUST, without hesitation, choose the hard way!

MY SON'S FINAL PLAYING DAYS

My son enjoyed playing baseball, but his abilities seemed like they peaked at ten. Like me at his age, he was smaller than everyone else. At twelve, he wasn't even five feet tall and competed against some six-footers. The strikes he threw, which made him a star when he was ten, were now "meatballs" that bigger kids were crushing. After his final season on the small diamond ended, he'd play one more season, this time in the Babe Ruth league on the big diamond.

I watched his games from the stands and then started umpiring more games. That year, I took classes to become a state-certified umpire, also known as "becoming patched." I was now qualified to umpire in all leagues for players nine to eighteen years old, including high school and legion games.

Once Dan stopped playing baseball, he started umpiring locally like I had. We umpired many games together, which was fun for both of us. He took the state certification classes when he was eligible at age eighteen and umpired all through college. He always had fun with the kids but, as a young umpire, endured a ton of grief from coaches and parents who tried to take advantage of inexperienced young umpires.

He warned me often that when college was over and he got a real job, his umpiring career would end. Upon graduation, he landed a good job and stopped umpiring at age twenty-two. It was a shame to lose an outstanding young umpire, which youth baseball desperately needs. Like so many others, he was driven away by adults behaving badly. He's now twenty-five, and while I'm still umpiring, he keeps reminding me how much he doesn't miss it!

WHEN LIGHT DAWNS ON MARBLEHEAD (FINALLY!)

Marblehead, Massachusetts, is a picturesque seaside community eighteen miles north of Boston. This coastal town is situated on a peninsula that extends into Massachusetts Bay. A common expression among New Englanders is said to have originated from a poet describing how the first light of a new day touches this piece of coastline.

The expression, "When light dawns on Marblehead," describes an "Aha!" or "Oh, now I finally get it!" moment, when, suddenly, someone "sees the light." They whack their forehead with the palm of their hand, and proclaim, "Duh! I'm so stupid, how could I possibly have not seen this before?" They now understand something that should have been obvious to them, but for whatever reason, just couldn't get it through their thick skull, or "marble head."

At some point, this revelation hopefully takes place with parents who thought their nine- or ten-year-old was a sure bet to be a professional baseball player. For years, they lived their lives as obnoxious parents, taking youth games way too seriously. Eventually, reality rears its ugly head and they finally realize that the child they love, who blinded them with his "talent" when he was younger, is, unfortunately, nothing special as a baseball player.

When my son played his final season of baseball at thirteen years old on the big diamond, we noticed that when players reached this age, the attitudes of many formerly obnoxious parents and ruthless coaches completely changed. There were a few exceptions, but most finally stopped taking the games so seriously. Suddenly, they "saw the light." As if by magic, the nonsense we'd seen for years in recreational league games involving players twelve and under practically vanished into thin air.

Parents did their job, sitting and watching the games. You hardly knew they were there. Nobody said anything to umpires other than "What's the count?" or "How many outs are there?" Coaches never barked at anyone or tried to pick fights with each other. Umpires rarely had to threaten to eject anyone. There was no drama. If a player made an error, or an umpire blew a call, it was no longer the end of life as we knew it. Everyone wanted their team to win but if they lost, it really didn't matter.

Finally, light had dawned on everyone's collective marble heads. For the first time, they "got it" and relaxed. It took years, but NOW they realized that it's just a bunch of kids playing baseball. Light dawns on the marble heads of many parents when their kids turn thirteen or fourteen. It's now apparent to them that the kid they thought was the next Pedro Martinez, David Ortiz, Mookie Betts, Aaron Judge, or Bryce Harper really isn't that much better than anyone else.

They've come to grips with the harsh reality that is life. The young star they were certain at nine years old had the talent to be a pro might not even make the high school team. As far as paying for college, they'd better get going on that college-savings plan, because recruiters offering scholarships aren't banging down their doors.

Having come back to earth, parents stop trying to relive their own failed childhood athletic fantasies through their children. They reluctantly accept that their teenager will have to go to college and then slug it out working the old-fashioned way like everyone else, because they won't be making a living playing baseball.

When adults finally realize and accept this, youth sports are better for everyone. It's fun for the parents. It's fun for the coaches. It's fun for the officials. Most importantly, it's fun for the players. "When light dawns on Marblehead," whether we're referring to a sunrise on that lovely stretch of the Massachusetts coastline or to adults no longer taking youth baseball way too seriously, it is truly a beautiful thing.

Unfortunately, some adults never "see the light," and as their young athlete becomes a teenager, they remain obnoxious. Parents of teenagers in town recreational leagues are usually more relaxed than they were when the players were younger, but that's not always the case in more competitive leagues, where bad adult behavior sometimes never ends.

By their nature, competitive club leagues are more focused on winning, and some overly competitive parents just don't let up. As their talented young athletes get older and enter high school, the poor behavior of parents remains an issue. It's a serious problem in high school sports, and the current shortage of officials is a crisis directly related to the abuse umpires and referees face. While some of the abuse officials deal with comes from coaches who are often under pressure to have winning teams, it more often emanates from parents of players.

In recent years, the MIAA, the governing body for high school athletics in Massachusetts, has tried to address the problem of inappropriate behavior by parents. They are also actively attempting to recruit people to become high school sports officials, as the shortage of officials continues to worsen. The lack of officials is a major problem in all sports nationwide, as veteran umpires and referees are resigning at a much faster rate than new officials are being recruited.

Poor adult behavior in youth sports starts when kids are young, and that's when it needs to stop. In youth leagues run by volunteers, parents are also the coaches. When kids are young and winning is all that matters to parents, especially those who also coach, a toxic atmosphere is created. The behavior of obnoxious parents and ruthless coaches becomes an accepted "part of the game" when players are young, and with some adults who only care about winning, it never ends. The wrong "life lessons" are being taught to players, and officiating games becomes so miserable for umpires and referees that we find ourselves in the situation we're in now, practically begging people to become youth sports officials.

What Bob Lemon said so many decades ago is still true, possibly more so than ever. Baseball is a game for kids, and grown-ups often do screw it up. We can stop the madness. Grown-ups can stop screwing it up. Parents need to just do their job, which at youth baseball games is to support their child's team without the extracurricular nonsense. Good, successful coaches know how to lead and encourage players to do their best. Coaches can still try to win but must stop themselves before they "cross the line." While trying to win, they must never forget how much players look up to them nor allow themselves to fall into the trap of becoming ruthless coaches whose only concern is their win-loss record.

The tales I've told are situations encountered in youth baseball by myself and fellow coaches, umpires, and parents. Undoubtedly, there are a million more stories out there. Whether they are funny, sad, strange, or bizarre, they all lead to the same conclusion.

Grown-ups take baseball and all youth sports way too seriously, and it needs to stop. Every game is not game seven of the world championships. Great people who coach and run youth sports programs volunteer so much time and energy for kids but screw it up when winning is all that matters to them. It's not all that matters to kids. What matters to kids is having fun, and when grown-ups screw it up, a lot of the fun goes away.

Baseball is an incredible game. Perhaps baseball was made for kids, but it has the power to make grown-ups feel like a kid again too. It doesn't matter if you're thirty, forty, fifty, or ninety. If you're a coach or a parent of a player, being involved in a baseball game and even just watching a game makes you feel like a kid again. What could possibly be more fun for anyone at any age than to feel like a kid again?

New England's head football coach Bill Belichick is famous for two things: First, for two decades, he's won a lot of football games and championships. Second, he's driven reporters crazy for the same two decades by never actually answering their questions. When asked to explain something, he often just shrugs his shoulders and utters something like, "It is what it is."

Youth baseball is what it is. It's a game for kids, and sometimes grown-ups screw it up. It should be 100 percent about the kids, not about their parents and coaches. Grown-ups need to stop screwing it up by making it about themselves. Baseball and all youth sports are great when they're simple and fun. Let's keep it that way, and just let the kids play.

GAME OVER... KIDS WIN!!

ACKNOWLEDGMENTS

My sincere thanks to the following people:

Brian Casey for your cover artwork and cartoons. Your talent never ceases to amaze me.

Denn Santoro and Helen Granger of High Road Marketing and Communications for your website design and support.

It's difficult for new authors, so thank you to the team at BookLogix for helping me cross "writing a book" off my bucket list!

Juri Love, author of *A Gift from Adversity*, for introducing me to BookLogix.

Lynda Loebelenz for introducing me to her friend, author Juri Love.

Foxboro, Massachusetts, youth umpire Erik Loebelenz, who umpired a game with me where his mom, Lynda, heard about my book and the trouble I was having finding a publisher.

Dan Shaughnessy, Brenda Hilton, and Dave Wallace for your endorsements of this book.

William Rigdon, who worked tirelessly with me to build a great youth umpire program; Brad McCreedy, who kept it going; and Barry Zimmerman and Norfolk Baseball for all your support.

My tech support staff, a.k.a. my kids, Jess Corwin and Dan Corwin, who did everything from setting up computers for me to stopping me from jumping off a bridge after I unintentionally moved paragraphs or made the entire manuscript vanish into thin air. I hope you inherit zillions someday from sales of this book, which I couldn't have written without your help.

My colleagues of the Central Massachusetts Baseball Umpires Association (CMBUA), "The Best in Blue."

Anyone who's ever worked as a youth sports official, which looks pretty easy until you try it.

Anyone who's ever volunteered their time as a coach, team parent, board member or in any other capacity to make youth baseball great, because it doesn't happen without all of you.

My readers, who I hope enjoyed reading this book as much as I've enjoyed writing it.

ABOUT THE AUTHOR

Lifelong Bostonian, Randy Corwin earned a BA in psychology from Southeastern Massachusetts University in 1977 and has a sharp, scathing sense of humor he was born with. He coached youth baseball for ten years before becoming an umpire in 2008. A member of the Central Massachusetts Baseball Umpires Association, he officiates games in recreational and competitive youth leagues, and lives with his wife, Janice, in Norfolk. This is his first book.

www.ingramcontent.com/pod-product-compliance
Lightning Source LLC
Chambersburg PA
CBHW020526080526
44583CB00013B/750